UNIX, *Quick!*

UNIX, Quick!

Andrew Feibus

PROFESSIONAL
PRESS BOOKS

Cover design by Michael Cousart

Trademark Acknowledgments

AT&T is a registered trademark of American Telephone and
Telegraph Company.
DESQview is a trademark of Quarterdeck Office Systems.
Hewlett-Packard and HP are registered trademarks and HP-UX is a trademark
of Hewlett-Packard Company.
IBM is a registered trademark of International Business Machines Corporation.
Microsoft is a registered trademark and Windows is a trademark of
Microsoft Corporation.
Sun Microsystems is a registered trademark and SunOS is a trademark of
Sun Microsystems Inc.
UNIX is a registered trademark of UNIX System Laboratories Inc., a wholly
owned subsidiary of AT&T.
VT and ULTRIX are trademarks of Digital Equipment Corporation.
X Window System is a trademark of Massachusetts Institute of Technology.

Library of Congress Cataloging-in-Publication Data

Feibus, Andrew, 1962-
  UNIX, quick! / Andrew Feibus.
     p. cm.
  Includes index.
  ISBN 1-878956-01-9 (pbk.) :
  1. UNIX (Computer operating system)   I. Title.
  QA76.76.063F42 1991   91-2183
  005.4'3—dc20   CIP

Please address comments and questions to the publisher:

Professional Press Books
101 Witmer Road
Horsham, PA 19044
(215) 957-1500 FAX (215) 957-1050
Internet: books@propress.com

This book is dedicated to
Jill and Justin Vogelhut,
Alison and Matthew Wender,
and Michael Feibus
with love
from Uncle Andy

Table of Contents

Chapter 7: Some User Utilities   137

Part III: UNIX, Quicker!   159

Chapter 8: Increasing Your vi
Editing Speed   161

Preface

In recent years, I've provided training for several different UNIX-based software products. Invariably, during the training class several people will share with me their frustrations with the UNIX operating system.

This UNIX stuff is so big, they say. DOS came with two small manuals; the UNIX manuals take up several bookshelves in my office. Where do I start? Is there some book that can help me?

Unfortunately, most UNIX books are either aimed too high (at programmers) or too low (at people who fear computers and the way computers are plotting to take over the world). Since many nonprogrammers already know and use DOS-based systems, these books don't help.

I used to tell these people that I knew of no book good enough to recommend and that the best course of action was to start with the *UNIX Reference Manuals* and try every command that looked interesting until, through perseverance, they had a grasp of some of the available commands.

However, this answer always felt very unsatisfying. (Actually, the answer stank, but let's not quibble about it.) Most people don't have the time to experiment with a new operating system but must contend with deadlines, productivity goals, performance targets, and other complex nouns that restrict available time.

Then, a few years ago, one person asked me for a list of the ten commands I used the most. After several minutes I handed him a list containing the fourteen commands I could recall using at least five times each week. I told him that learning these commands would allow him to obtain information from the system and to demonstrate the system to others.

Those commands became the basis for the first technical article I wrote for publication. The article was published in the February 1989 issue of *HP Professional* magazine. *HP Professional* also published subsequent articles that assist new users with learning the important features of UNIX. Since *HP*

Professional has a limited circulation, many new UNIX users are probably still struggling to learn the operating system.

So this book is for you, the DOS user who wants to be able to use a UNIX system without struggling and wasting a lot of time learning UNIX commands and utilities that you will never use.

This book is divided into three parts:

Part I provides new users with the bare minimum required to get into the system and do some quick editing. It also provides a bit of background information to make the operating system less mystical.

Part II is for users who want to spend a little time learning to take advantage of certain UNIX features. This section, a little more complex than Part I, contains useful information for anyone likely to spend more than an hour each day using the system.

Part III covers some advanced topics for anyone who will spend much of their time using a UNIX system. The information in this part shows how to decrease the time you spend doing repetitive tasks.

I considered a few different implementations of UNIX when writing this book. The two systems I used for testing all examples were Hewlett-Packard's HP-UX Version 7.0 and Santa Cruz Operation's UNIX System V/386 Version 3.2. Within the context of this book, both operating systems are very similar to AT&T UNIX System V Release 3. I also verified as many examples as possible on Sun Microsystems' SunOS Version 4.1 and on Digital Equipment's ULTRIX Version 4.0.

I investigated the changes made for UNIX System V Release 4 and noted any major discrepancies in the text. The biggest difference between the two releases is the organization of the system directories. All examples in this book use the Release 3 directory organization, since this organization corresponds to most of the implementations of UNIX now available. The differences between the Release 3 and Release 4 directory organization are discussed in Chapter 2.

Only AT&T and its licensees can market a product named "UNIX." Other software and hardware vendors claim that their operating systems are compatible with UNIX; these other operating systems are what I call *versions* or *implementations* of UNIX. These operating systems are not UNIX; however, they are popular enough and similar enough that they deserve some mention, although not necessarily by name. In general, this book sticks to the generic AT&T UNIX System V.

If your specific implementation of UNIX does not coincide with the examples in this book, refer to your documentation for clarification.

One more thing: Some of the humor in this book may confuse certain readers. If you're one of them, don't worry: my family doesn't understand me either.

Acknowledgments

Many people helped and influenced me during the creation of this book. These people and their contributions are listed here.

Thanks to Annette Nelson of Professional Press, my editor for this book. My huge phone bills reflect how much fun it was to work with you.

Thanks to Tom Halligan and Andrea Zavod of Professional Press for providing me with the opportunity to write about UNIX on a monthly basis. One of these articles in particular was the inspiration for this book.

Thanks to the rest of the folks at Professional Press who had a hand in the creation of this book.

Much love to Laurie Katz, my friend for more than ten years! Your critique of my initial draft and enthusiasm for the entire project were greatly appreciated.

Many thanks to my parents and to my brother, Stephen, for proofreading the initial draft and providing insights.

Finally, this book would not have been done without the love, support, and encouragement of my family: Mom, Dad, Sharon and Stephen, Stephen and Michelle, and Judy and Steve. Thank you.

Conventions Used in This Book

Certain conventions are used throughout this book:

❏ UNIX commands, which are case-sensitive, UNIX filenames, and UNIX directories are in `letter gothic` typeface.

❏ UNIX shell variables, shell parameters, and control variables are italicized.

❏ DOS commands, such as COPY, are shown in small caps.

❏ References to keyboard keys, such as the BACKSPACE and ENTER keys, are in capital letters.

❏ In example sessions with the computer, the ENTER key is also referenced as the RETURN key, and is shown as ⏎ .

❏ The ESCAPE key is usually referred to as the ESC key.

❏ The character generated by simultaneously holding the CTRL key and pressing another key (for example, Z or C) is a control character. In text, control characters are shown as the string "CTRL" followed by a hyphen and the key, such as CTRL-Z. In example sessions with the computer, control characters are shown as the circumflex (^) followed by the key, such as ^Z. Note that you should not type the letters "CTRL," but should press and hold the CTRL key and the character key to complete the control character.

❏ In examples in which the location of your terminal's cursor is important, the cursor is shown as an underscore (_).

❏ In the example sessions with the computer, the commands or responses you type are in `letter gothic` typeface and are highlighted in color. If you are to press the ENTER key, it is indicated by a ⏎ . The computer's response to your entry is in `letter gothic` typeface but is not in color.

Part I

Getting Acquainted with UNIX

You are about to confront the unknown head-on. A new operating system. UNIX. You know it's different. After all that time you spent learning DOS, now you have to learn another one.

The worst part is that it came with 50 pounds of documentation. DOS wasn't like that: It had one manual for the commands and another for BASIC. Life was much simpler then.

Now what? Where do you start? What can you do? *Where's the on/off switch?*

Forget the on/off switch. Concentrate on understanding where to find information in the manuals and on learning some of the more useful UNIX commands.

Onward....

Chapter 1

Getting Started

FIRST, YOUR MANUALS

In general, the UNIX operating system includes five to seventy-five pounds of documentation. Most of it is pretty bad. The worst part about the UNIX documentation is that the information you need may be located in three different manuals and completely obscured by technobabble.

The basic UNIX system is normally bundled in one of two ways:

❑ As a minimal system for users only

❑ The complete development system

The minimal system usually includes a description of the installation procedure, an administrator's guide, a user's guide, and the *UNIX Reference Manual*. The *UNIX Reference Manual* may have a different title if your version of UNIX has a different name. For example, Hewlett-Packard's HP-UX version of UNIX includes an *HP-UX Reference Manual*. The *UNIX Reference Manual* frequently is divided into several binders or books, sometimes titled the *User's Reference Manual* and the *Programmer's Reference Manual*.

The development system usually includes a programmers guide, a C language guide and reference manual, an assembler manual, a debugger manual, a libraries manual, and extra sections of the *UNIX Reference Manual*.

The *UNIX Reference Manual* is intended to provide a description of every command, subroutine, and file format in the standard UNIX system. This manual, also known as *the brick*, is the most important manual you will use.

Pick up your *UNIX Reference Manual*. Notice that it is separated into sections that (depending on the version of UNIX) are either numbered 1 through 7 plus 1M or named C, ADM, S, M, and F. Each section contains a particular type of information, as listed in Table 1-1.

Table 1-1. Sections of the UNIX Reference Manual

Type of Information	Numbered Section	Named Section
Commands that may be executed by any user	Section 1	Section C
Core UNIX subroutines for programs the user writes	Section 2	Section S
Subroutines in the standard C libraries, and graphics libraries, etc.	Section 3	Section S
Commands that only the system administrator may execute	Section 1M	Section ADM
Formats for files used by standard UNIX utilities	Section 4	Section F
Device files used to communicate with external peripherals such as tape drives	Section 7	Section F
Miscellaneous information not found in other sections of the manual; for example, how to specify the time zone of your system	Section 5	Section M

If your UNIX system was shipped without any programming capabilities, you may not have Section 2 or Section 3 (or Section S).

By the way, Section 6 once contained the documentation for games. Unfortunately, most UNIX systems no longer include games.

Each entry in this manual covers a single command or concept. An independent entry, also called a *manual page*, or a *manpage*, may contain one or more pages. All entries in each section are ordered alphabetically, except for an intro entry, which is sometimes placed at the beginning of each section.

Included with the manual is an index for locating the entries related to a particular topic. The index is the most important tool for finding information in your UNIX manuals.

In the UNIX manuals, references to commands are appended with the number or name of the section containing the description of the command. For example, in the expression `ls`*(1)*, the number *1* in parentheses indicates that the documentation for `ls` is in Section 1 of your *UNIX Reference Manual*. This book adheres to this convention.

NOTE: You may be confused by the similarity between the lowercase letter l and the number 1. All commands discussed in this book begin with a letter, not a number.

Spend a few minutes to skim through the entries in Section 1. This book regularly refers to the information in Section 1.

As you can see, hundreds of commands are included with the standard UNIX system. Don't worry. As with DOS, you will use fewer than 13 user commands more than 90 percent of the time.

However, before using any UNIX commands, you must get onto the system.

GETTING STARTED

Sit down in front of your UNIX terminal. If your terminal is on and properly connected to the UNIX system or host, the following message is on your screen:

```
login: _
```

If your screen is blank, press the ENTER key (RETURN or ↵) two or three times. If your screen remains blank or displays unintelligible information, ask your system administrator for help.

If you are on a system with a graphical user interface (for example, the X Window System), your login message may appear slightly different from the one shown above; however, the intention of the graphical message is the same as the terminal-based message.

The login message is the first major difference between a DOS-based system and a UNIX-based system. DOS is designed to accommodate only one user at a time; UNIX is a multiuser system.

Multiuser systems provide each user with a separate environment in which to work. The environment also is known as an *account*. Users gain access to a UNIX system by requesting to access a particular account.

Each account is identified by a username or account name assigned by the system administrator when the account is created. In UNIX jargon, this name is also the *login name*, because it is entered in response to the `login:` prompt.

WARNING: Unless otherwise specified, do not use the account *root* while performing any of the examples in this book. This account has special privileges that are not available to standard user accounts.

Your administrator must tell you the name for your account. To begin using your account, enter your login name in response to the `login:` or equivalent prompt.

NOTE: Your CAPS LOCK key must not be active when you type your login name. Login names are case-sensitive and are usually composed of lowercase letters.

Press ENTER once you have entered your login name; like DOS, UNIX requests and responses are issued by pressing the ENTER key.

On some UNIX systems, you cannot use the BACKSPACE key to back up and correct an error in your login name. You must correctly type your UNIX login name when prompted or the system will request it again.

To restrict unauthorized access to your account, your administrator may have assigned a password to the account. If so, after you enter your login name, the following prompt appears:

```
password: _
```

Your administrator should have told you what password was assigned to your account. Enter your password at this time. Do not use the BACK-SPACE key while entering your password. Notice that while you enter your password, what you type is not displayed. Remember to press the ENTER key once you have typed the password string.

If you have incorrectly entered either your login name or your password, the system displays the following:

```
incorrect password
login: _
```

Enter your login name and password again. If you continue to have trouble, ask your administrator for assistance.

NOTE: To increase security, UNIX systems respond the same when you enter the wrong password as when you incorrectly enter your login name; in both instances you will receive the `incorrect password` message and get another prompt for your login name.

Your administrator may not have assigned an initial password to your account. Instead, the administrator may configure your account to force you to assign a password the first time you access it. In this case, after entering the login name, the system prompts with this:

```
Your password has expired.
Enter new password: _
```

Enter a password consisting of a memorable string of uppercase characters, lowercase characters, and numbers.

Some systems restrict the password string; if your system enforces a restriction and if you enter a password that fails these restrictions, the system again prompts you for a password. Once you enter an acceptable password string, the system requests that you confirm it by entering it again.

When you have properly responded to the login and password prompts, you are logged in to your account. Most UNIX systems display several messages at this time. For example:

```
Welcome to your UNIX System v4.0
Logging in at Tue Jul 5 12:20:42 EDT 1989
```

The actual messages depend on how your system and your account are configured. After these login messages is another prompt, which may be either

```
$ _
```
or
```
% _
```

or possibly something else. This *shell prompt* is similar to the prompt string issued by COMMAND.COM on DOS systems.

For most of this book, a $ precedes each command that you enter. You should not type this $; it indicates that the computer is waiting for you to enter a command. Many examples in this book are concluded by

```
$ _
```

This line indicates that the final command in the example has completed and that the computer is expecting another command. Since the example has ended, you need not enter anything more.

WHERE ARE YOU?

When you have successfully logged on, UNIX automatically places you in your *home directory*. Your system administrator determined your home directory's location when creating your account.

The actual name of your home directory is not important yet. At present you need to know only that your home directory provides a unique area for any files or directories you create.

Most other users on the system cannot access the files you might create in your home directory (or in any directory you create within your home directory). In general, changes you make to the files in your directory do not affect other users.

YOU SAID, "MOST OTHER USERS..."

Your system administrator has access to the *superuser* account. The superuser account name is usually *root*. The superuser account can access and affect all files, programs, and activities on the system. Consider the superuser account to be the UNIX system deity.

This information is provided merely to explain why your system administrator is always busy.

You are now ready to begin executing commands.

SOME SIMPLE COMMANDS

The most common DOS command is DIR, which displays a list of the files in the current directory. On UNIX systems this command is 1s*(1)*. Remember that the *(1)* indicates that documentation for this command can be found in Section 1 of the UNIX *Reference Manual*.

NOTE: Unlike DOS, UNIX commands are case-sensitive. DOS commands use uppercase and lowercase letters interchangeably. All DOS commands in this book are shown using uppercase letters. All standard UNIX commands use lowercase letters only.

To execute `ls`, enter the command when your shell prompt is displayed. For example:

```
$ ls ⏎
```

The $ is your shell prompt; do not enter this character. The command, `ls`, is shown in bold typeface to indicate that you entered this command, and the ⏎ indicates that you must press the ENTER (or, on some keyboards, RETURN) key to execute the command.

Because your account is new, the `ls` command probably displays no files. Don't worry about it: the night is young.

Like DOS, every UNIX directory provides the special filenames . (the current directory) and .. (the parent directory). Unlike the DIR command, however, these special files are not displayed by the `ls` command unless you include the `-a` (to list all) option:

```
$ ls -a ⏎
.
..
.profile
$ _
```

In the above example, lines two through four show a possible response from the `ls` command. See Chapters 5 and 6 for a discussion of the file `.profile`.

However, `.profile` demonstrates one very important difference between DOS and UNIX: UNIX filenames are not restricted to eight characters with a three-character extension. On most UNIX systems, filenames may contain at least 14 characters; some systems permit filenames to contain as many as 256 characters.

UNIX does not reserve characters for filename extensions: Any extension you place on a filename is considered to be part of the name. In other words, `h1.doc` is a filename that contains six characters, not two characters plus a three-character extension.

UNIX does not require a filename extension. However, some UNIX tools, for example, the C programming language compiler, may require you to use filename extensions. For example, a word processor may ask you for a document name, to which you enter *letter1*. When this document is created and accessed, the program may use the file *letter1.txt;* the use of the extension *.txt* is enforced by the tool (the word processor) but not by UNIX.

In general, UNIX filenames that begin with a dot are configuration or initialization files for UNIX programs and utilities. For example, .profile is an initialization file for the Bourne shell; more on the Bourne shell shortly. Files beginning with a dot are not shown unless you include the option -a in the command ls.

As you may have observed from the ls example, UNIX command options have a different format from DOS command options. DOS command options begin with the slash (/), and UNIX options begin with the minus sign (-). As with DOS commands, more than one option may be specified for UNIX commands.

For example, to list all information about all files in the current directory, use options -a (all) and -l (long) for ls:

```
$ ls -l -a ↵
total 6
drwxr-x---  2  amf   users  64   Apr 27 11:19 .
drwxrwxrwx  5  root  other  384  Jan 21 10:22 ..
-rw-------  1  amf   users  539  Apr 27 11:19 .profile
$ _
```

The ls command provides much more information about a file than does DIR. For a discussion of the information that ls displays, see Chapter 2. This example only demonstrates how to specify UNIX command options.

Most UNIX commands permit you to precede a set of options with a single minus sign. For example, the command in the above example could have been entered as ls -la.

Another common DOS command is COPY, which copies files from one location to another. The UNIX copy command, cp(1), has similar arguments. For example, to copy the file /bin/true to your current directory, use the command:

```
$ cp /bin/true . ↵
```

Unlike COPY, cp requires a destination. In the example, the period specifies your current directory as the destination for the copy. Now when you execute ls, your directory reveals:

```
$ ls ↵
true
$ _
```

The DOS RENAME command is the same as the UNIX mv(1) command. To rename true to almost_true, do the following:

```
$ mv true almost_true ↵
```

Now a directory listing shows:

```
$ ls
almost_true
$ _
```

Another frequently used DOS command is DEL (or ERASE), which erases the specified file or, if a wildcard is used, a set of files. The UNIX equivalent for this command is rm(1). To erase almost_true from your directory, enter this command:

```
$ rm almost_true ↵
```

Now you know the UNIX commands equivalent to the four most frequently used DOS commands. Remember that 13 UNIX user commands are used more than 90 percent of the time.

WHAT ARE THE OTHER NINE?

Just in case you're wondering, the other nine most frequently used UNIX user commands, listed alphabetically and not in order of use, follow:

cd	Change directory
kill	Terminate a program
lp	Spool/print a file
man	Display the on-line manual
mkdir	Create a new directory
pg, more	View a file page by page

ps	Display the current status of all running programs
pwd	Display the current directory location
vi	Full-screen editor

All these commands are documented in Section 1 of your *UNIX Reference Manual* and in Part I of this book.

If you are a programmer, your list of frequently used commands may include cc, make, ar, ld, and lint. These commands are beyond the scope of this book.

ONLINE DOCUMENTATION

Most UNIX systems include online documentation that is exactly the same as the information in the *UNIX Reference Manual*. To access the online documentation, use the man(1) command.

For example, to view the online documentation for ls, use this command:

```
$ man ls ↵
```

The manual entry is displayed page by page on your screen. The end of each page shows either the : or –More– prompt. If the prompt is :, press ENTER to view the next page. If the prompt is –More–, press the space bar to view the next page.

On some UNIX systems, disk space is scarce, and the online documentation may not be installed. If either man reports no manual entry for ls or you receive the message

```
man: No such file or directory.
```

you should ask your system administrator for an explanation.

SOME TOPICS NOT TO WORRY ABOUT

Two topics that all DOS users worry about are memory usage and concurrently running more than one program.

DOS programs requiring more than the standard 640 kilobytes (KB) must resort to extended or expanded memory. If the program is not designed to use these tricks, the program will probably crash and require you to restart your computer.

Stop worrying. UNIX was designed to take advantage of as much memory as you can install in your computer. UNIX programs are not concerned with the amount of memory in your computer: That responsibility lies with the operating system.

As you probably know, DOS is not designed to permit concurrent program execution or *multitasking*. Some products provide multitasking for DOS programs; however, you have to buy additional software, and these products may not cooperate with your favorite program.

UNIX is a multitasking operating system. No additional software is required to permit more than one user to execute any number of programs concurrently. UNIX provides this feature.

UNIX also prevents any program you might run from crashing the system. So don't worry! You really can't harm the system.

Chapter 2 contains a detailed discussion of UNIX memory and multitasking capabilities.

WHERE IS THE ON/OFF SWITCH ?

Because UNIX computers are normally used by more than one person at a time, you should not turn off (shut down) your system when you are finished working with it.

However, once you are finished using the system for the day, you should leave (or log out of) your account. To log out, type:

```
$ exit ⏎
```

But don't leave so quickly. You've just gotten started.

Chapter 2

The UNIX File System

DISKS AND THE FILE SYSTEM

The DOS file system is divided into multiple independent disk partitions. These partitions are accessed using a letter followed by a colon (for example, C:).

Each DOS partition contains a set of files in an inverted tree directory structure beginning with the directory \. A specific partition is chosen to be active, and the system tries to boot from this partition.

Figure 2-1 illustrates a sample DOS file system. In this figure, each floppy and hard disk contains its own directory structure.

Figure 2-1

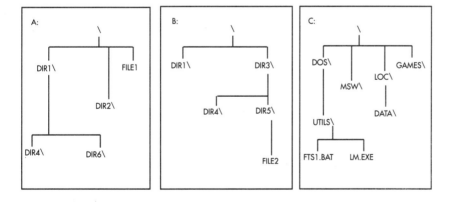

The UNIX file system contains a single inverted tree directory structure regardless of the number of physical disks connected to the system.

One of the physical disks is the *root disk*, and it contains an inverted tree directory with a top-level directory named /. The / directory also is known as the *root directory*. All other physical disks connected to your UNIX system are accessed as subdirectories of the / directory.

Figure 2-2 shows a sample UNIX file system containing several disks. In this figure, disk1 contains the root directory and disk2 is accessed from the directory /usr.

Figure 2-2

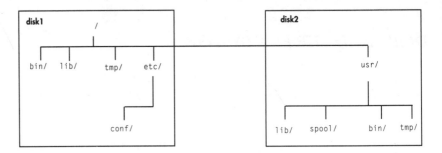

DOS uses the backslash (\) to separate the directories specified as part of a filename; UNIX uses the slash (/). For example, /usr/bin refers to the directory bin in the directory usr, which is in the root directory.

NOTE: As with commands and account names, UNIX filenames are case-sensitive.

ORGANIZATION OF THE UNIX FILE SYSTEM

Unlike DOS, which permits you to organize your disks any way you please, the UNIX file system is organized into a standard directory structure. A portion of the System V Release 3 directory structure is pictured below:

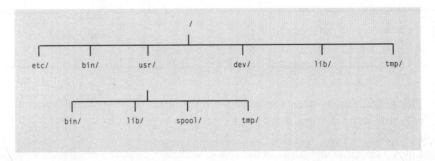

Each name in this structure is followed by a / to indicate that the name is a directory. Not all standard UNIX directories are included in this picture;

some standard directories are four or more levels below the root directory (for example, /usr/lib/terminfo/a).

The files contained in each directory shown in this example are described below:

/etc/ — All system administration commands, configuration files, and installation control files.

/bin/ — The core set of system commands and programs. Most systems cannot boot (initially start) without executing some of the commands in this directory.

/dev/ — The device files used to access system peripherals (for example, your terminal can be accessed from /dev/tty). Chapter 3 contains more information on device files.

/lib/ — The standard set of programming libraries linked with all UNIX programs.

/tmp/ — Temporary files created and used by many UNIX programs.

/usr/bin/ — The majority of the noncritical UNIX user commands.

/usr/lib/ — The nonstandard libraries (for example, graphics libraries) and the control files for certain system tools (some of which are described in Chapter 7).

/usr/spool/ — The control files for certain system facilities, including the printer spooler, electronic mail, and system-to-system communications.

/usr/tmp/ — More temporary files created and used by programs.

Under UNIX System V Release 4, the directory organization looks like this:

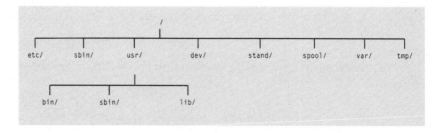

The contents of the directories are described below:

/etc/ — The system administration and configuration databases. The system administration utilities are in /usr/sbin.

/sbin/ — The system programs used to boot the system and perform any system recovery. This directory is similar to /bin in release 3.

/dev/ — The device files directory, similar to /dev in release 3.

/stand/ — The standard system programs and data files required to boot your UNIX system.

/spool/ — Similar to /usr/spool in release 3.

/var/ — The directory containing all files that vary from UNIX system to UNIX system, including files for logging system activity and storing electronic mailboxes (see Chapter 7).

/tmp/ — The same as in release 3.

/usr/bin/ — The same as in release 3.

/usr/sbin/ — All system administration utilities.

/usr/lib/ — All libraries for programs and programming languages.

For all examples in this book, the release 3 directory structure is used, since release 4 is not prevalent. If your implementation of UNIX uses the release 4 directory structure, refer to your manuals for the locations of specific commands and files.

Let's Explore

To begin exploring the file system, you need to know one more command: cd(1). This command is similar to the DOS command CD, which lets you change your current directory.

For example, to change your current directory to /usr/lib, enter the command:

```
$ cd /usr/lib ←┘
$ _
```

For practice, use ls(1) to list the files in this directory. To change back to your home directory, use cd:

```
$ cd ←┘
$ _
```

Executing cd with no arguments differs from CD in DOS. CD with no arguments displays the current directory name. To display the current directory name in UNIX, use pwd(1).

For example, if you are in your home directory, using pwd results in:

```
$ pwd ←┘
/users/amf
$ _
```

My home directory is /users/amf; your home directory will have a different name.

To create a directory, use mkdir(1), which is the same as the DOS command MKDIR. To create the directory work1 in your home directory, do the following:

```
$ cd ←┘
$ mkdir work1 ←┘
$ _
```

An ls of your home directory reveals:

```
$ ls ←┘
work1
$ _
```

To remove a DOS directory, you must first remove all files in the directory with ERASE or DEL and then remove the directory with RMDIR. UNIX removes both files and directories with the rm(1) command. With rm, you can also remove a directory and its files with a single command.

To remove a directory and any files and subdirectories in it, use the -r option for rm. The -r option specifies that file removal is recursive; all files and all directories in the specified locations are removed.

For example, let's copy a file into work1 and then remove both work1 and the file in work1. First, copy the file into work1:

```
$ ls ⏎
work1
$ cp /bin/true work1 ⏎
$ ls work1 ⏎
true
$ _
```

Now see what happens if you try to remove the directory work1 without using -r:

```
$ rm work1 ⏎
rm: work1 directory
$ ls ⏎
work1
$ ls work1 ⏎
true
$ _
```

Now, let's remove the directory and its files with the -r option:

```
$ rm -r work1 ⏎
$ ls ⏎
$ _
```

As you can see, both work1/true and work1 were removed by the rm command, but only if the -r option was included. You can remove individual files without specifying -r. However, you can never remove a directory without including -r.

CAUTION: Unlike DOS, UNIX does not automatically ask, "Are you sure?" when you remove all files in a directory.

If you want rm to request confirmation when you delete a file, specify the
-i option (interactive). Let's rerun the previous example and include the
-i option:

```
$ ls ⏎
work1
$ cp /etc/true work1 ⏎
$ ls work1 ⏎
true
$ rm -ir work1 ⏎
directory work1: ? y ⏎
work1/true: ? y ⏎
work1: ? y ⏎
$ ls ⏎
$ _
```

For each directory that rm -ir encounters, rm first asks whether to proceed
into that directory. In the example, this question is "directory work1: ?". If
you answer y (yes), rm enters that directory and removes any files in it (after
querying you about performing the deletion). Once all the files in a directory
are deleted, rm asks whether you want to delete the directory itself (in the
example, work: ?). As with DOS, the directory cannot be deleted if there are
any files in it.

The best way to learn about the UNIX file system is to use cd and ls to explore. First, though, you may need some additional information about ls.

Some UNIX systems provide a single column of output for the ls command;
some provide a multicolumn tabular output. If your version of ls displays
files in a single column, you can obtain multicolumn output by including
the -C option (for example, ls -aC).

When you use ls without the -l option to provide a long list, you cannot
determine which files are programs and which files are directories. Another
way to provide this information is the -F option. For example:

```
$ ls -aFC ⏎
./    ../    .profile    true*
$ _
```

In this example, . and .. are directories, which is indicated by the / after their
filenames. The file true is an executable program, and is so indicated by the
* after the filename in the output. The file .profile is neither an executable

program nor a directory, so `ls` does not append an indicator to it.

Time to go exploring. Come back when you get bored and want to know how to view the contents of these files.

VIEWING UNIX FILES

To view the contents of text files, UNIX System V Release 3 provides two programs, cat(1) and pg(1). Use `cat` to display files of less than one page. To view a longer file one page at a time, use the pager program `pg`. Most implementations of UNIX, in addition to System V Release 4, include another pager: more(1).

For example, to view the contents of the file `/etc/profile`, you can do the following:

```
$ cat /etc/profile ←
```

The `cat` program, like the DOS command TYPE, is good for viewing files containing less than one terminal screen of text. For longer files, `cat` does not pause between terminal screens of text.

NOTE: The `cat` program has many more uses. In its simplest form, `cat` copies the contents of a file to the terminal. See Chapter 3 for other uses.

To view the file page by page, use `pg`:

```
$ pg /etc/profile ←
```

At the bottom of each page, `pg` pauses and displays this prompt:

```
:
```

Press ENTER to view the next page. Press the minus sign followed by ENTER to redisplay the previous page. Press H then ENTER to display other available commands. To terminate `pg`, enter Q.

Personally, I prefer more(1) to `pg`:

```
$ more /etc/profile ←
```

At the bottom of each page, `more` pauses and displays a prompt like this:

```
—More—(32%)
```

The number in parentheses indicates the amount of the file you have displayed. At this prompt you have several options:

❏ Press the space bar to view the next page.

❏ Press q to terminate more.

❏ Press ⏎ to view the next line of the file.

❏ Press v to begin editing the file at the current page. Don't try this option yet.

❏ Type / followed by a string of characters and press ENTER; more will locate the next occurrence of the string and continue displaying the file from this location.

❏ Type :p to view the file (again) from the beginning.

❏ Type ! followed by a command and press ENTER to cause more to execute the command before continuing. Try entering !ls -a at the prompt.

You may use more (or pg) to view more than one file at a time. For example:

```
$ more /etc/profile /etc/inittab ⏎
```

When the −More− prompt is displayed, you may type :n to view the next file in the list. In the example, while you are viewing /etc/profile, type :n to begin viewing /etc/inittab.

Editing is covered in Chapter 4, so don't press v at the −More− prompt just yet. The choice is mentioned to demonstrate that the UNIX version of more is more powerful than DOS MORE or UNIX cat.

An attempt to use more to view a program returns an error message:

```
$ more /bin/ls ⏎
******** /bin/ls: Not a text file ********
$ _
```

UNIX may not let you view the contents of a particular file. For example:

```
$ more /etc/passwd ⏎
/etc/passwd: permission denied
```

Don't worry about this message yet. UNIX permissions are discussed next.

FILE PERMISSIONS

All UNIX files are assigned a set of file permissions on creation. There are three types of permission—*read*, *execute*, and *write*—and three levels of permission—*owner* (the creator of the file), *group*, and *world*.

Owner permissions determine the activities permitted by the owner of the file. File ownership may be changed by chown(1); however, this command is usually restricted to the system superuser.

Group permissions determine the activities permitted by members of a user group. The system administrator may assign a user account membership in one or more user groups. One of these groups is the user's *primary group*. When a file is created, the creator's primary group is selected as the file's group. A file's group may be changed by chgrp(1); however, only the file's owner or the superuser may use this command.

World permissions determine the activities permitted by users who are neither the file's owner nor in the file's group.

How are permissions determined for each level? Let's go back to an example from Chapter 1:

```
$ ls -1 -a ⏎
total 6
drwxr-x---   2      amf     users   64      Apr 27  11:19 .
drwxrwxrwx   5      root    other   384     Jan 21  10:22 ..
-rw-------   1      amf     users   539     Apr 27  11:19 .profile
$ _
```

Notice the third and fourth columns in the example. The third column reports the name of each file's owner (amf, root, and amf, respectively). The fourth column reports each file's group—users, other, and users, respectively.

The fifth column, highlighted below, displays the size for each file (in bytes):

```
drwxr-x---   2      amf     users   64      Apr 27  11:19 .
drwxrwxrwx   5      root    other   384     Jan 21  10:22 ..
-rw-------   1      amf     users   539     Apr 27  11:19 .profile
```

The next column shows the last time the file was modified:

```
drwxr-x---   2   amf    users   64    Apr 27  11:19 .
drwxrwxrwx   5   root   other   384   Jan 21  10:22 ..
-rw------:    1   amf    users   539   Apr 27  11:19 .profile
```

The first column of ls -l output reports the type of file and its permissions:

```
drwxr-x---   2   amf    users   64    Apr 27  11:19 .
drwxrwxrwx   5   root   other   384   Jan 21  10:22 ..
-rw-------    1   amf    users   539   Apr 27  11:19 .profile
```

This column always contains 10 characters separated into four sets:

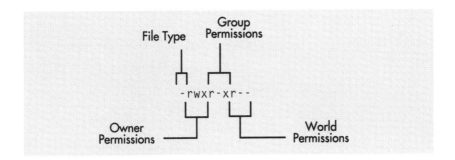

Table 2-1 lists the meaning indicated by each set.

Table 2-1. Character Numbers and Meanings

Character Number	Meaning
1	The type of file. Common values are - (regular file) and d (directory). In addition, the following types of files are also available: p (a named pipe, beyond the scope of this book); c (character device; e.g., a terminal); b (a block device; e.g., a disk); and l (a symbolic link to another file). Symbolic links are discussed later in this chapter; device files are discussed in the next chapter.
2-4	Permission set for the file's owner.

Table 2-1. Character Numbers and Meanings (continued)

Character Number	Meaning
5-7	Permission set for the file's group.
8-10	Permission set for all users who are neither the file's owner nor a member of the file's group.

Each permission set is composed of three characters, as shown below:

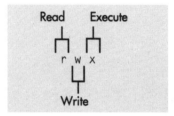

The first character reflects the file's read access for the set. If this value is r, the file may be read by the users having this permission. If it is -, the file may not be read by these users.

The second character reflects the file's write access for the set. The value is either w (it may be written to) or - (it may not). This permission also controls deletion of the file or directory.

The third character reflects the file's execute (or search) access for the set. This value is either x (may be executed), s (may be executed with certain additional priveleges), or - (may not be executed). For regular files, this permission usually indicates that the file is a program. Directories with execute access allow those users to cd into (search) the directory. Named pipes and device files do not use this permission.

Take another look at ls -l -a:

```
$ ls -l -a ⏎
total 6
drwxr-x---   2      amf     users   64      Apr 27  11:19  .
drwxrwxrwx   5      root    other   384     Jan 21  10:22  ..
-rw-------   1      amf     users   539     Apr 27  11:19  .profile
$ _
```

In this example:

❑ The current directory, shown as the file . on the third line of the example, may be accessed in any manner by the directory's owner (amf); other members of group *users* may read information from this directory, but may not write or create anything in it; no other users on the system may access this directory.

❑ The parent directory (. .) may be accessed by all users for any activity.

❑ The file .profile may be read and written to only by user amf. No other users on the system may access this file. This file contains 539 characters and was last modified on April 27 of this year. If the file had last been modified in a previous year, the year would be shown instead of the time in this column of the output.

An example of a file with execute permission is /bin/ls:

```
$ ls -l /bin/ls ⏎
-r-xr-xr-x  6 bin   bin     31070  Jun 18 1989  /bin/ls
$ _
```

This file is executable by all users, as indicated by the x in all three permission sets. Certain administration utilities have a special execution setting, indicated by a permission of s for either the owner or group. When a program with this execution permission is run, it inherits the privileges provided to either the owner of the program or the program's assigned group (determined by the permission set in which the s appears).

This concept is best shown by the following example:

```
$ ls -l /usr/bin/lp ⏎
---x--s--x  2 bin   lp      91364  Jun 24 1989  /usr/bin/lp
$ _
```

In this example, when /usr/bin/lp executes, it inherits the privileges of group lp. In effect, when you run this program, you temporarily inherit the privileges of the group lp (in addition to your normal privileges).

The advantage to this permission is that the program is allowed to read from and write to files and directories accessible to group *lp* (which you may not normally be allowed to access). This type of execution is used mostly by administrative programs such as passwd(1), which changes your account password, or system facilities such as lp(1), which is discussed later in this chapter, and cron(1), which is discussed in Chapter 7.

Changing File Permissions

To change the permissions for a file that you own, use chmod(1). The *UNIX Reference Manual* provides specifics, but here are a few examples.

To add read permission for all users to .profile, do the following:

```
$ chmod +r .profile ⏎
```

To add group-write permission to all files in your directory containing the suffix .c, enter this command:

```
$ chmod g+w *.c ⏎
```

The * wildcard, similar to the DOS * wildcard, is discussed in Chapter 3. To change the permissions for all files in your directory containing the suffix .f to permit (only) reading and writing by you and members of the file's group, do this:

```
$ chmod u+wr *.f ⏎
$ chmod g+wr *.f ⏎
$ chmod o-wr *.f ⏎
$ chmod -x *.f ⏎
```

The u in the first line of the example indicates the owner permission set. The o in the third line of the example indicates the world permission set. Not specifying a particular permission set implies that the change occurs to all three permission sets.

You could have performed the above example in one step using numbers to indicate each set of permissions. Use the following table to translate each permission set into a single digit:

```
--- = 0
--x = 1
-w- = 2
-wx = 3
r-- = 4
r-x = 5
rw- = 6
rwx = 7
```

To repeat the exercise using these numbers, you would use the single command:

```
$ chmod 660 *.f ⏎
```

The numbers 660 translate into `rw-rw----`, which was the effect of the four `chmod` commands.

Who Cares about File Permissions?

Now that you've waded through all of this information, what was the point? Remember the example from earlier in this chapter?

```
$ more /etc/passwd ⏎
/etc/passwd: permission denied
```

Why could `more` not view `/etc/passwd`?

```
$ ls -l /etc/passwd ⏎
-r--------   1 root  other   231 Jun 10     1989  /etc/passwd
```

Because `/etc/passwd` is readable only by root, and you are not user root so you cannot view the contents of this file.

WARNING: If you are using the root account: **STOP! DO NOT USE THE ROOT ACCOUNT UNLESS YOU ARE PERFORMING ADMINISTRATION TASKS!**

How UNIX Determines File Permissions

How does UNIX decide what permissions to assign to a file you create? When you use `cp` to copy an old file, by default, the permissions on the new file are the same as on the original. When a new file is created, all users are granted unlimited access to the file by default.

You can, however, automatically restrict certain permissions with the `umask(1)` command. With `umask`, you select permissions to always remove from any files you create.

The syntax for using `umask` is

```
$ umask mode ⏎
```

where *mode* is a number describing the permissions to remove from any file you will create. The number is composed the same way that you would use numbers to assign a file's permissions with `chmod`. These numbers were discussed a few paragraphs back.

If you want to prevent all other users from writing into files you create, use the command:

```
$ umask 022 ↵
```

The numbers 022 translate into the permissions ----w--w-. These permissions are automatically removed from any files you create when the command is executed.

One more note about UNIX file permissions: Each user and group name corresponds to a unique user and group identification number, respectively. This correspondence is determined when the system administrator creates the account and group.

To determine your user identification number (uid) and primary group identification number (gid), use the command id(1). For example:

```
$ id ↵
uid=240(demo1) gid=50(users)
$ _
```

In the above example, user account demo was assigned uid 240 and primary group users, which is gid 50. For user root, the id returns:

```
$ id ↵
uid=0(root) gid=1(other)
$ _
```

All user accounts are assigned a unique uid number. On UNIX systems the root account is always assigned uid 0.

FILE LINKING

When you use cp to copy a file, you create a duplicate of the entire file. Each copy reserves additional space in your file system and may be modified independent of the other copies.

Sometimes, you need to access the same file with several filenames. For example, you might want to access a single data file from more than one directory. What you need to create is a *link* to the file.

To create a link, use the ln command. For example, to create a link named dir in the current directory to the file /bin/ls, enter the following:

```
$ ln /bin/ls dir ↵
$ _
```

A link is an additional directory entry that refers to a single file. Remember the discussion of `ls -1`?

```
$ ls -l /bin/ls ↵
-r-xr-xr-x  6 bin   bin      31070  Jun 18  1989  /bin/ls
```

The second column shows the link count for the file; in this example the link count, 6, specifies the number of links created for a single file. Each link is indistinguishable from the original file.

Now, if you look at your copy of `dir`, you will see this:

```
$ ls -l dir ↵
-r-xr-xr-x  7 bin   bin      31070  Jun 18  1989  dir
```

The two files look the same except for the name. Which file is the original? It doesn't matter. Each link points to the same file. Using `rm` to remove `dir` does not affect `/bin/ls` except to decrease the link count by one.

The problems with this scheme are that:

1. You cannot easily tell which files are linked to which other files.

2. You cannot create a link to a directory.

3. You can create links only between files on the same physical disk. If you have a system with more than one disk, this limitation is not very convenient.

Symbolic Links

To overcome the limitations of the standard link, many versions of UNIX, including Release 4, include *symbolic links*. A symbolic link is an actual file that is a pointer to another file. To create a symbolic link, use the `-s` option for `ln`:

```
$ ln -s /bin/ls dir1 ↵
$ ls -l dir1 ↵
lrwxrwxrwx  1 amf   users    6          Apr 18  10:45  dir1 -> /bin/ls
$ _
```

In this example, `dir1` is a symbolic link to `/bin/ls`. The link file has a file type of `l` (indicating it is a link), has different permissions than `/bin/ls`, and is just large enough to keep its link information. Because `dir1` is a pointer to

/bin/ls, accessing dir1 is the same as accessing /bin/ls:

```
$ dir1 -a ⏎
.
..
.profile
dir1
$ _
```

The symbolic link does not increment the link count for /bin/ls. The disad-
vantage to a symbolic link is that removing the original file silently invali-
dates the symbolic link because the file that the symbolic link points to is
no longer present.

You can also identify a symbolic link using the -F option on the ls command:

```
$ ls -Fa ⏎
.
..
.profile
dir1@
$ _
```

The @ indicates that dir1 is a symbolic link. Also, if you use rm to remove a
symbolic link, you affect only the link file and not the original file.

PRINTING FILES

DOS systems, because they are single-user systems, do not have a standard
way to manage multiple printing requests. UNIX systems provide lp(1) not
only to manage multiple print requests to a single printer, but to manage
more than one printer running at the same time.

To print a set of files using lp, use the command

```
$ lp files ⏎
```

where *files* are the names of the files to print, separated from one another by
one or more spaces. In most instances, a form-feed character is sent to the
printer between each file to separate the files.

When printers are attached to the system, each printer is assigned a name.
Printers also may be grouped into a class. Print jobs destined for a

particular class are routed by lp to the first idle printer in the class.

One printer is usually designated as the default printer; print jobs without a specific printer destination are automatically routed to the default printer. A class of printers also may be chosen for a default printer destination.

To print the file /etc/profile on printer lp1, do the following:

```
$ lp -dlp1 /etc/profile ⏎
request id is lp1-194 (1 file)
$ _
```

The option -d (destination) specifies the name of a particular printer or a printer class to perform the print job; in the example, the destination is printer lp1. The response message from lp indicates the request identification number for the print job and the number of files to print. More on this identification number in a moment.

To print multiple copies of each file, use the option -n. For example, to print three copies of /etc/inittab on the default printer:

```
$ lp -n3 /etc/inittab ⏎
request id is lp0-290 (1 file)
$ _
```

You may have noticed in the above two examples that the options required secondary arguments, the name of the printer or the number of copies. Options with secondary arguments should not be combined. In this instance, the two options cannot be combined with a single minus sign. You cannot use both -d and -n without separating them. Compare

```
$ lp -n3 -dlp2 files1 ⏎
```

to

```
$ lp -dlp2n3 files2 ⏎
```

The first command will print three copies of files1 on printer lp2. The second command would attempt to print a single copy of files2 on printer lp2n3, which may not exist.

Print Request Status

To determine the status of any print jobs remaining in the system, use lpstat(1). For example:

```
$ lpstat ⏎
lp0-292      amf      2338    Apr 27  11:36   on lp0
$ _
```

Without options, `lpstat` displays only your print jobs that have not completed. To display the status for all print jobs in the system and the status for the printers, use the `-t` option:

```
$ lpstat -t ⏎
scheduler is running
system default destination: lp0
device for lp0: /dev/lp
device for lp1: /dev/lp1
lp0 accepting requests since Thu Aug 3 09:29:26 1989
lp0 accepting requests since Thu Aug 3 09:29:27 1989
printer lp0 now printing lp0-292. enabled since Thu Aug 3
09:30:23 1989.
printer lp1 is idle. enabled since Thu Aug 3 09:30:23 1989.
lp0-292      amf      2338    Apr 27  11:36   on lp0
```

Normally, only system administrators use the `-t` option. Users would use it to determine why a print job did not complete. For example, if a printer has been disconnected for repair, the status may appear like this:

```
$ lpstat -t ⏎
scheduler is running
system default destination: lp0
device for lp0: /dev/lp
device for lp1: /dev/lp1
lp0 accepting requests since Thu Aug 3 09:29:26 1989
lp0 accepting requests since Thu Aug 3 09:29:27 1989
printer lp0 disabled since Fri Apr 27 11:39:03 1990. Printer
maintenance
printer lp1 is idle. enabled since Thu Aug 3 09:30:23 1989.
lp0-292      amf      2338    Apr 27  11:36   on lp0
$ _
```

The `lpstat` command is used for two primary reasons: to find out why a print job has not completed and to provide you with the request identification numbers for your outstanding print jobs. The request identification number is required to cancel a print job.

If a print job has not completed, you may cancel it (even if it is being printed) by using the cancel(1) command. For example, to cancel the print job with request identification number lp1-234, use the command:

```
$ cancel lp1-234 ⏎
request "lp1-234" canceled.
$ _
```

TIME TO PRACTICE

Spend a few minutes practicing using links, printing files, and working with file permissions. When you are comfortable with the ideas in this chapter, go on to Chapter 3.

Chapter 3

Processes and the Shell

This chapter discusses the UNIX concepts of shells and processes. Before you can fully understand a process, however, you must understand the philosophical differences between DOS and UNIX.

THE _REAL_ DIFFERENCE BETWEEN DOS AND UNIX

So far in this book, you have learned two things: UNIX commands and some DOS equivalents, and where to find information in the heap of UNIX manuals.

As you might have suspected, UNIX is different from DOS in more ways than just the number of available standard programs. This section discusses some of these differences, from the standpoints of philosophy and implementation.

Single-User Versus Multiuser Systems

DOS is a single-user system; unless you purchase additional software (for example, Microsoft Windows or Quarterdeck Office Systems' DESQview), DOS is a single-tasking system as well. A single-tasking system is capable of executing only one program at any time. In a single-tasking system all peripherals (such as printers) and system resources (such as memory) are dedicated entirely to the current task.

Although certain DOS programs, such as hot-key programs, can reside in memory and execute when a certain event occurs (for example, when a keyboard key is pressed), these programs are the exception to the DOS single-tasking rule. The basic rule is that you cannot, in a normal DOS system, run two programs at the same time without additional software.

UNIX, on the other hand, is a multiuser, multitasking operating system capable of executing any number of tasks simultaneously. The UNIX _kernel_ manages all the different tasks and their resources. The kernel starts when the UNIX system is booted.

Some of the responsibilities of the UNIX kernel include the following:

❑ Handling output to and input from disks and other system peripherals. Unlike DOS applications, UNIX programs do not need to understand each peripheral's communications requirements.

❑ Managing the way the system's physical memory is allocated to tasks that are executing.

❑ Arbitrating conflicts between tasks requiring the same system resource.

❑ Managing other system resources, such as pipes, which are described later in this chapter.

Most UNIX systems contain only one central processing unit (CPU), so only one program can actually execute at any time. You can start any number of programs, however, and UNIX controls when these programs execute.

The process of determining when tasks can use the CPU is called *task scheduling* and is another function of the UNIX kernel.

"But," you may say, "you can run multiple programs using Microsoft Windows. What makes UNIX better?" Keep reading.

UNIX tasks are scheduled to use the CPU based on a priority that is continuously adjusted by the kernel for all programs running in the system. The kernel's algorithm for adjusting priorities automatically lowers the priority for a task that requires large amounts of CPU time, favoring interactive tasks.

If more than one task is waiting for the CPU, the task with the highest priority runs the next time the CPU is available. Each task can use the CPU for only a predefined period (time slice) before the kernel automatically stops it and starts the next task waiting to use the CPU.

On certain implementations of UNIX, you can request a particular priority for a task and prevent the kernel from adjusting this priority. This is usually called *real-time UNIX*.

Under DOS, the above scheme doesn't exist; but, then again, single-user, single-tasking systems don't need complex schemes. Besides, no one ever needs to run more than one program at a time, right? Sure.

Memory Usage

Another difference between DOS and UNIX is in the way memory is managed and allocated to programs that are executed.

Way back in the Dark Ages, DOS (and the Intel Corp. 8088 chip set of the original personal computer) was designed to access a maximum of 640 kilobytes (KB). At the time, this size was considered huge, because most programs could run on 64 KB.

Well, it's now a decade later, and DOS can still only access 640 KB, but many programs now require more than one megabyte (MB) of memory. To overcome this limitation, some programs take advantage of the extended memory or expanded memory standards, either of which permit (with restrictions) programs to access memory beyond the 640-KB limit. However, only certain programs use them. Even if extra memory is available, neither technique ensures that a program can obtain enough memory to operate.

UNIX, on the other hand, is a (buzzword alert!) virtual memory operating system. The principles behind a virtual memory operating system are that:

❑ Only a small amount of memory is in use at any time by a particular program. In other words, only a small section of the code is being executed at any time, and this code references only a small section of the program's data.

❑ Regardless of the amount of physical memory available, each program assumes it can access as much memory as it requires. The amount of memory the program can access, determined by the kernel, is usually no less than 16 MB.

A virtual memory operating system loads into the system's physical memory (the random access memory, or RAM) only the sections of code and data that are being executed or referenced at a particular moment. The rest of the program and data area is stored on a portion of a system disk known as the *swap area*.

The swap area is configured when the system disks are installed. The swap area must be larger than the memory requirements for all programs to be running at any given time. For example, if programs AB, BD, and DC are all to run at the same time, the swap space must be large enough to store the combined code and data areas for AB, BD, and DC.

When a program is loaded and before it begins to execute, its initial memory requirements for code and data are reserved in the swap area and the contents of the program file are copied to the swap area. When the program begins to run, its initial sections of code and data are copied from the swap area to the system's physical memory.

This transference is called *paging*, since the information is copied in chunks of memory called pages, usually between 512 bytes and 8192 bytes of code or data. The transference also is known as *swapping*.

UNIX programs also can dynamically request more memory from the system; when this happens, the system allocates more swap space to the program.

When a program needs a section of code or data that is not in physical memory, the kernel transfers the required section into physical memory. Once physical memory is completely full, no RAM is available for receiving the requested page. The kernel must then remove, or swap out, one or more pages from memory to accommodate the request.

The kernel usually removes the page or pages least recently used by any program. This algorithm is the most efficient for most programs.

If the contents of the page have changed, for example because its data has been modified, the page is copied back to the swap area. The kernel then loads the requested page into physical memory.

So, the more physical memory you have installed in the system, the less swapping your programs require. Swapping is time-consuming. Each swap can require as little as thirty milliseconds or more than one second, depending on how much swapping must be performed to accommodate the request and on the speed of the disk containing your swap area.

Finally, unlike DOS, UNIX programs may access all of the memory available within the system without using some "bolted-on" memory standard.

Now you have something to chat about during your coffee break.

THE SHELL

The UNIX shell is the program (similar to COMMAND.COM) that prompts you for commands to execute. A shell is operational as long as you are logged on to the system. The commands you execute may be programs such as `ls` and `more` or special commands recognized only by the shell. The special shell commands are discussed in Chapters 5 and 6.

Two shells are commonly found on UNIX systems: the Bourne shell (`/bin/sh`) and the C shell (`/bin/csh`). Some UNIX systems include a third shell, the

Korn shell (/bin/ksh). Each shell has different capabilities. To determine which shell you are using, enter the command

```
$ echo $SHELL ⏎
```

The shell returns either /bin/sh, /bin/csh, or /bin/ksh, depending on which shell you are using. The echo(1) command provides a way of displaying text and other information.

This book discusses only the Bourne shell and the C shell in depth. Because of the Korn shell's limited availability and staggering complexity, this book discusses it only superficially. However, since the Korn shell contains features derived from both the Bourne shell and the C shell, you should review the information provided for both of these shells if you plan to use it.

The actions of a shell are similar to the actions of COMMAND.COM. The shell indicates it is ready by displaying its prompt, usually $ _ or % _. When you type a command, the shell interprets the command string and executes the request. If a command string requests a program to be run, the operating system loads and starts the program. When the program completes, the shell prompts you for another command.

You may execute more than one command from a shell by separating the commands with a semicolon. For example, to execute ls and then more /etc/profile, you could enter:

```
$ ls; more /etc/profile ⏎
```

If multiple commands are specified as a single shell request, the commands are executed from left to right on the line. You may wonder why you would want to execute more than one command in this fashion. One reason is shown later in this chapter.

Chapters 5 and 6 discuss tailoring your shell and shell programming, respectively. The next section covers shell configuration variables.

Shell Variables

Under DOS you may SET certain variables to provide information used by certain programs. However, no standard variables are defined for all DOS applications, and DOS does not assign default values to any variables when you start COMMAND.COM.

When you start a UNIX shell, it automatically defines certain shell variables to provide information to programs about your account. You may assign other shell variables once you have logged in to the account.

Shell variable names are case-sensitive; *VAR1* is not the same variable as *var1*. All shells use the following variables:

HOME — This variable contains your home directory, from which you start when you log in to your account.

SHELL — Your shell's program location; for example, /bin/csh.

PATH — Similar to DOS, the *PATH* variable defines the directories that the shell searches when you specify a program to execute.

LOGNAME — Your account name; the name you typed in response to the login: prompt.

The following shell variables, discussed later in this book, are used by many UNIX programs:

TERM — The type of terminal you are currently using. For example, if you are using a Digital Equipment VT100, you should assign vt100 to this variable. Before you can do any full-screen editing (see Chapter 4), this variable's value must reflect the type of terminal you are using.

TZ — The time zone. The value for this variable is usually set by the system administrator.

EDITOR — The program to use as your default editor.

To view the value for a shell variable, use the echo(1) command

```
$ echo $var  ⏎
```

where *var* is the name of the shell variable. The shell requires that a dollar sign precede the variable name when you request its value. For example, to view the value for *TERM*, enter the command:

```
$ echo $TERM  ⏎
```

The assigning of a value to a shell variable is shell-specific. If you are using the Bourne shell, use the syntax

```
$ var=value  ⏎
```

where *var* is the name of the shell variable to assign and *value* is the new value for this variable. For example, to assign vt100 to *TERM*, use:

```
$ TERM=vt100 ←
```

If you are using the C shell and you want to assign vt100 to *TERM*, enter the command:

```
$ setenv TERM vt100 ←
```

Chapter 5 contains more information on shell variables.

Shell Wildcards

As with DOS, you may use wildcard characters in arguments for UNIX programs to specify a set of files. For example, to select all files with the suffix .BAS, use the string *.BAS. Like DOS, two UNIX wildcard characters are * (match any number of characters) and ? (match a single character).

The major difference between UNIX and DOS wildcard usage is that DOS wildcards are interpreted by DOS commands and UNIX wildcards are interpreted by the UNIX shell. This means that, in DOS, only certain commands may be able to interpret wildcard characters; the UNIX shell interprets all wildcard characters before the program is started and all filenames matching the wildcard specification are passed as arguments to the program.

To understand this difference, consider the DOS TYPE command, which copies the contents of a file to your screen. Assuming that C> is your DOS prompt, attempting to display the contents for all files in the current directory with a .TXT suffix produces this:

```
C> TYPE *.TXT ←
Invalid filename or file not found
C> _
```

The error message is returned because TYPE does not interpret wildcard specifications. However, in UNIX you can execute this:

```
$ cat *.txt ←
```

If the current directory contains the files al.txt, a2.txt, and a3.txt, that command is exactly the same, from cat's perspective, as this one:

```
$ cat al.txt a2.txt a3.txt ←
```

Another difference between DOS and UNIX is that UNIX wildcards may appear anywhere within a filename specification. For example, to indicate all files ending with _rt, use *_rt; DOS does not permit this type of filename specification.

UNIX wildcard specifications also provide a way to match a single character from a set of characters. To specify a set of characters, enclose the set of characters with square brackets. For example, to match all files beginning with any of the letters A, B, D, G, H, K, P, and Z, use the specification [ABDGHKPZ]*.

This may look difficult if you want to specify all lowercase characters between a and z, but this case is covered by specifying a range of characters to include in the set. Ranges are specified by separating the first and last characters in the range by a minus sign (-). For example, instead of using ls -a to display all files in the current directory beginning with a period, use:

```
$ ls .[a-zA-Z]*+  ⏎
```

This example demonstrates that any number of ranges may be included in a set. Ranges are determined based on the ordering stated in ascii(5).

Why isn't

```
$ ls .*  ⏎
```

the same as

```
$ ls .[a-zA-Z]*  ⏎
```

Because the file specification .* matches not only all files beginning with a period but also the current directory and the parent directory, and listing the contents of these directories was not intended.

PROCESS INPUT AND OUTPUT

When a program is run, it is called a *process*. Each UNIX process automatically opens three standard files:

stdin — Standard input is the location from which the program expects to obtain input. The default stdin location is the keyboard attached to the terminal from which the program was started.

stdout — Standard output is the location to which the program expects to route information and user prompts. The default stdout location is the screen on the terminal from which the program was started.

stderr — Standard error is the location to which the program expects to route error and warning messages. The default stderr location is the screen on the terminal from which the program was started.

Figure 3-1 illustrates the relationship between a process, stdin, stdout, and stderr.

Figure 3-1

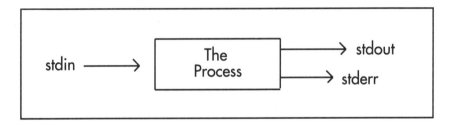

Unlike UNIX programs, DOS programs automatically open and use stdin and stdout, but not stderr.

Unless files are explicitly selected, most UNIX commands request input from stdin and all output is sent to stdout and stderr. For example, in Chapter 2, the cat(1) command was shown to copy the contents of a file to the screen (similar to TYPE). Actually, cat copied the contents of the file to stdout, and stdout's default location is your terminal.

You also may use cat to copy the contents of stdin to stdout; this feature is selected by specifying a - as the name of the file to copy. For example:

```
$ cat - ⏎
hello there ⏎
hello there
^D
$ _
```

In this example, cat copies the contents of stdin (the keyboard) to stdout (the screen). You entered the text "hello there," which the program read from stdin. When you press ENTER, the line you entered is copied to stdout and displayed on the terminal.

Use the CTRL-D key combination to indicate the end of the input; when `cat` detects the end of the input (whether input is from stdin or a file), it terminates.

The following example demonstrates how stderr is used:

```
$ cat /etc/goop ⏎
cat: cannot open /etc/goop: No such file or directory
$ _
```

In this example, the file /etc/goop does not exist. The error message is sent to stderr, which by default displays the message on the terminal's screen. Mostly, you will not need to use output from stderr until you begin shell programming. See Chapters 6 and 9 for shell programming and Chapter 5 for more on stderr.

Redirection

Each of the standard files discussed above has a default location. For example, the default location for stdin is the terminal keyboard. Both DOS and UNIX allow you to change these locations using a technique called *redirection*. The term *redirection* is used because the input or output is redirected from its default location to another location.

To redirect stdin, causing a program to receive its input from a file instead of the keyboard, use the syntax

```
$ command < file ⏎
```

where *command* is any program that obtains input from stdin and *file* is the name of a file from which any requests for input can be satisfied. For example, another way to use `cat` to view the contents of the file /etc/profile is:

```
$ cat - < /etc/profile ⏎
```

Although the above example seems silly (you could have used the command `cat /etc/profile` instead), other examples are shown later in this chapter to demonstrate some of the power of stdin redirection.

To redirect stdout to a file, use the syntax

```
$ command > file ⏎
```

where *command* is any command that routes output to stdout and *file* is the file to which output from *command* is routed. For example, to place the date and time (from the date(1) command) into the file stat, enter the following:

```
$ date > stat ↵
```

To append a command's stdout results to the end of a file, use the following syntax:

```
$ command >> file ↵
```

For example, to add a list of the files in /bin to stat:

```
$ ls /bin >> stat ↵
```

Stdin and stdout can be independently redirected for a single command. The following example redirects stdin from one file and redirects (and appends) stdout to another:

```
$ cat - < /etc/inittab >> glomp1 ↵
```

All stdin and stdout redirection described above is available within DOS; however, most DOS programs do not take advantage of these capabilities. Most UNIX programs are designed to use stdin and stdout.

With redirection, you can use cat to create text files. This is worse than using the DOS editor EDLIN, but helps to understand stdin and stdout. The following example illustrates:

```
$ cat - > textfile ↵
This is example text entered into the file textfile. ↵
On the way to the end of this file is the ↵
last line, as always, to be written. ↵
^D
$ cat textfile ↵
This is example text entered into the file textfile.
On the way to the end of this file is the
last line, as always, to be written.
$ _
```

Pipes
Many times you will want to use the output (stdout) from a program as the

input (stdin) for another. Both DOS and UNIX provide *pipes* to perform this action.

A pipe's function is to route stdout from one command to stdin of another. The syntax for piping *command1* into *command2* is:

```
$ command1 | command2 ⏎
```

This concept is illustrated in Figure 3-2.

Figure 3-2

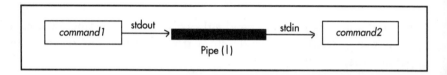

On most keyboards the pipe symbol (|) is on the same key as the backslash (\). The commands on both sides of the pipe execute simultaneously. An example of how to use pipes:

```
$ ls -l /etc | more ⏎
```

This command displays a listing of the files in the /etc directory page by page. The output from ls (with the -l option to create a long listing) is piped into the more command, which displays the results one terminal screen at a time. The way more is used in this example is similar to the way the DOS MORE command is used. The example is similar to using the DOS DIR command with the /P option.

You can also route the output from multiple commands either to a single file or into a pipe. For example:

```
$ (date; ls -l /etc ; cat /etc/inittab) | more ⏎
```

This command pipes all output generated by the commands date, ls, and cat into more. The parentheses are required to provide grouping; if the parentheses were not there, only the output from the cat command would have been piped into more.

The result is to display — one terminal screen at a time — the date, the list of files in the /etc directory and the contents of the file /etc/inittab. Without the parentheses, the date and the list of files in /etc are displayed without stopping at the end of each screen and only the contents of /etc/inittab is displayed page by page.

More Process Input and Output

In order to continue the discussion about process input and output, you need to know two more commands:

grep — Search for a string of characters, reporting each line containing the string. For a case-insensitive search, use the -i option. To display only the names of the files in which the string appears, use the -l (list) option.

wc — Count the number of lines (-l option), words (-w option), or characters (-c option).

Both commands, which are documented in Section 1 of the *UNIX Reference Manual*, obtain their input either from stdin or from files and route their output to stdout (and errors to stderr).

Pipes route the stdout from one program to stdin of another program. What if you want to use the stdout from one program as the arguments of another? UNIX shells provide this capability with the following syntax:

```
$ command1 `command2 `⏎
```

The delimiters about *command2* are grave marks and are usually found on the same key as the tilde (~). *Command2* is executed first. The results routed to stdout are used as arguments for *command1*, which executes when *command2* completes.

Let's say you have a group of text files in your current directory. To count the number of words in each file that contains the string "Copyright", do the following:

```
$ wc -l `grep -l Copyright *` ⏎
```

The command grep -l Copyright * reads all files in the current directory and reports the name of each file containing the string "Copyright." Let's say that grep reports the files textfile1, loclnes, guppytoe, and the_type. The wc command is then executed as though you had entered:

```
$ wc -l textfile1 loclnes guppytoe the_type ⏎
```

Just too cool for words, huh?

KEEPING TRACK OF PROCESSES

When a program starts and becomes a process within the system, UNIX assigns a process identifier (PID) number to it. UNIX uses PID numbers to track each command executed. A PID number is a unique (within the system) positive number not larger than 32,767.

To view what processes are running and their respective PID numbers, use the ps(1) command. Without options, ps displays only processes you are executing. Right now, since you are not executing anything, this listing would be dull.

Two ps options are frequently used: -e (display every process that is running) and -f (display a full listing for each process). To view a full listing for every process now running:

```
$ ps -ef ⏎
   UID   PID  PPID  C    STIME TTY       TIME COMMAND
   root    0     0  0   Apr 10  ?        0:00 sched
   root    1     0  0   Apr 10  ?        0:02 /etc/init
   root    2     0  0   Apr 10  ?        0:00 vhand
   root    3     0  0   Apr 10  ?        0:01 bdflush
    amf  257     1  2 11:21:48  01       0:03 -sh
   root  168     1  0 11:13:32  02       0:01 /etc/getty tty02
   root  169     1  0 11:13:32  03       0:01 /etc/getty tty03
   root  145     1  0 11:13:28  ?        0:00 /etc/cron
   root  170     1  0 11:13:32  04       0:01 /etc/getty tty04
   root  151     1  0 11:13:30  ?        0:01 /usr/lib/lpsched
   root  171     1  0 11:13:33  05       0:01 /etc/getty tty05
   root  172     1  0 11:13:33  06       0:01 /etc/getty tty06
    amf  303   257 19 11:32:28  01       0:00 ps -ef
 $ _
```

The names of the running programs are reported in the last column of each line of output from the ps -ef command. The user who started the program is reported in the first column of each line. The PID number is reported in the second column. The other columns are not important for this discussion; refer to your *UNIX Reference Manual* if you are interested.

One other ps option that is frequently used is -a; use this option to view all processes started by users of your system, including you:

```
$ ps -af ⏎
```

```
UID    PID  PPID  C    STIME TTY      TIME COMMAND
root   221   169 12 11:21:48  02      0:03 ls -R
amf    304   257 19 11:32:40  01      0:00 ps -af
$ _
```

The -f option without the -e or -a lists only the processes associated with
your terminal.

CONTROLLING A PROCESS

Programs are started either in *foreground* mode or in *background* mode. The
shell waits for foreground programs to terminate before prompting for another command. Programs that are candidates for background mode are
those that:

❏ Take a long time to run

❏ Do not require input from your keyboard

❏ Do not route too much output to your terminal

By default, all programs begun from a shell execute in foreground mode.
To execute a program in background mode, append an ampersand (&) to
the command.

You can create a list of all files in your system by using the -R (recursive)
option of the ls command. To create this listing in background mode, do
the following:

```
$ ls -R / > filelist1 & ↵
2918
$ _
```

The response line from the shell contains the PID number for each background process created; in this example, the PID number is 2918. You may
run other commands while the background process executes.

If you want to place more than one command — either separated by a
semicolon or connected by a pipe — in background mode, group the commands with parentheses and place the ampersand after the closing parenthesis. For example, to count the number of files in /etc, you could execute:

```
$ (ls -l /etc | wc -l) > list.out & ↵
```

```
3017
$ _
```

The result is placed into the file list.out in the current directory. To interrupt and terminate a process, use the kill(1) command. For example, to terminate the process with PID number 2918, enter:

```
$ kill -9 2918 ⏎
```

The -9 option causes kill to immediately terminate a process. Other options are possible; however, in most instances you should use -9.

UNIX also provides the nice(1) command to let you lower the priority of a process that requires large amounts of CPU time. You also should lower the priority for any background tasks you start before you go home for the evening.

MISCELLANEOUS ACTIVITIES USING REDIRECTION

I wanted to cover these topics in Chapter 2; however, you first needed to understand redirection. Now that you do....

Formatting Your Files for Printing

If you have attempted to use your printer, you are aware that lp(1) does not format your files for printing. Fortunately, lp, like cat, also accepts input from stdin. And UNIX just happens to include the utility pr(1), which formats text files and writes the formatted output to stout.

If you're not sure how these two utilities can be used together, reread the section in this chapter on pipes before continuing.

With pr, you can:

❑ Use the -h option to place special headings at the top of each page of output or use the -t option to eliminate any heading

❑ Use the -l option to define the number of lines you want placed on each page

❑ Use the -o option to indent all text by a specific number of spaces

❑ Use the -n option to place a line number before each line of text

For example, to print two copies of listing1 with line numbers, the standard pr heading (which contains the name of the file and the time of the file's last change), and only 55 lines of text on each page, use the following:

```
$ pr -n -l55 listing1 | lp -n2 ⏎
request id is lp0-292 (standard input)
$ _
```

Device Files

A *device file* lets UNIX communicate with any external peripheral. For example, UNIX accesses your disk drives with a disk drive device file. UNIX systems group all device files in the /dev directory.

All terminals on your system also are accessed from device files, called *ttys*. To learn which device file corresponds to your terminal, use the tty(1) command:

```
$ tty ⏎
/dev/tty02
$ _
```

In this case, the device file used to access your terminal is /dev/tty02. You can use this knowledge and the echo command to display a message on your terminal:

```
$ echo "Hello" >/dev/tty02 ⏎
Hello
$ _
```

This example routes the word "Hello" to the device file, which displays the information on your terminal.

Another important device file is /dev/null, which also is known as the *UNIX bit bucket*. Redirect output to this device if you do not want it; the device reads the information and does nothing with it. The bit bucket is used in some of the examples included later in this book.

Setting Up Your Terminal

As already discussed, part of setting up your terminal is configuring the *TERM* shell variable. Another part is configuring the data communications line with stty(1) to match your terminal's characteristics.

The stty command is similar to the MODE command for COM1 or COM2; that is, it establishes a line speed and parity for a serial communications line. However, since UNIX serial communications lines interpret some of the data being received and transmitted, stty must provide control over more line characteristics than just speed and parity.

Some of the characteristics configured with stty include line speed and parity handling, backspace key handling, and BREAK handling. To view all of the current characteristics set for your terminal, use the -a option for stty:

```
$ stty -a ⏎
speed 9600 baud;  swtch = ^@; susp = ^Z;
intr = ^C; quit = ^\; erase = ^H; kill = ^U; eof = ^D; eol = ^@;
-parenb -parodd cs8 -cstopb hupcl cread -clocal -loblk -ctsflow -rtsflow
-ignbrk brkint ignpar -parmrk -inpck -istrip -inlcr -igncr icrnl -iuclc
ixon ixany -ixoff
isig icanon -xcase echo echoe echok -echwnl -noflsh -iexten -tostop
opost -olcuc onlcr -ocrnl -onocr -onlret -ofill -ofdel tab3
$ _
```

This listing, however cryptic it may seem, lists the 50 or so characteristics of your terminal. Each characteristic in the first two lines is terminated by a semicolon; more than one choice is possible for each of these characteristics. The fields in the last five lines are separated by a space and each field usually has only two settings, on and off.

The fields in the output preceded by a minus sign indicate a control that is off; all other control fields are on. In the above example the control *ignbrk* is off. All of the fields in the stty command are documented in the *UNIX Reference Manual*; a few of the important ones follow:

ignbrk — Ignore the BREAK key. To accept BREAK key handling, set this control to off.

brkint — The BREAK key can interrupt a program running in foreground when this control is on. You must set this field on and ignbrk to off if you want to use the BREAK key to interrupt the programs you run.

erase — Defines the key used to backspace. On most terminals this key is either CTRL-H (the BACKSPACE key) or the DELETE key.

echoe — When on, the erase key (defined by the erase field) generates a backspace-space-backspace sequence, which erases the previous character on the line.

echo — When on, what you type is echoed to the terminal. Unless this field is on, you cannot see what you type. On some systems, the shells automatically set this field to on when the shell prompt is displayed.

intr — Defines a key that sends an interrupt to the program running. Most people use CTRL-C. If you don't have a BREAK key, this key defines how you can interrupt your programs.

kill — Defines the key that erases the entire line just typed. This key is similar to using the erase key to erase all characters typed on the line.

speed — Defines the data communications speed for your terminal.

parenb — When on, parity checking is enabled for the communications line.

parodd — When parenb and parodd are on, odd parity checking is performed on the data communications line. When parenb is on and parodd is off, even parity checking is performed.

tab3 — Expands tabs into the appropriate number of spaces.

To change the characteristics for your terminal's communications line, use the `stty` command with the specified field (either with a minus to turn off the control or without a minus to turn the control on). To turn off ignbrk and turn on brkint, enter:

```
$ stty -ignbrk brkint ⏎
```

To set one of the control characters, specify the field followed by a character:

```
$ stty intr \^C ⏎
```

For command arguments, you can represent a control character in one of two ways: as a two-character sequence containing a backslash, followed by the control character (for example, \CRTL-Z) or as a three character sequence containing a backslash, followed by a circmflex and a letter (for example, \^Z). In most cases, use the three-character sequence to specify a control character as a command argument. To change the speed of your terminal's communications line to 1200 baud, enter:

```
$ stty 1200 ⏎
```

WARNING: Do not change your communications line speed without immediately changing your terminal's speed to match the new line speed.

It's good to issue this `stty` command whenever you log on:

```
$ stty erase \^H intr \^C tab3 -ignbrk brkint echoe ⏎
```

This command sets your erase character to the BACKSPACE key, the interrupt character to CTRL-C, establishes useful tabs, makes the BREAK key send an interrupt (the same as CTRL-C), and makes the erase key visibly remove the previous character on the line.

By the way, if a program you run changes your communications line's settings and you can't run `stty` from your terminal, you can run `stty` from another terminal and change the settings for your communications line. For example, to improve (but not entirely correct) the settings for the terminal associated with `/dev/tty02`, use:

```
$ stty sane < /dev/tty02 ⏎
```

The sane keyword provides adequate (but not the best) settings for your terminal's communications line. Once this `stty` command has been run, the terminal should be usable but still acting slightly strange; other `stty` commands may now be run from your terminal to completely reset the communications line.

You can also save your terminal's communications line settings in a file by using the `-g` option on `stty`:

```
$ stty -g >default.stty ⏎
```

Once this file has been created, you can reset your `stty` settings with:

```
$ stty `cat default.stty` ⏎
```

This command causes the contents of `default.stty` to be used as the arguments for `stty`. Pretty nifty, huh?

EXERCISES

You should spend time now to experiment with the commands and concepts discussed in this chapter. Specifically, concentrate on:

❑ `pr` and `lp`

❑ `stty`

❑ redirection of stdin and stdout

❑ pipes

When you want to learn how to edit files, continue with Chapter 4.

Beginning to Edit

DOS provides EDLIN, a line-oriented editor providing very few features. DOS users invariably purchase a word processor to do any serious editing.

The primary UNIX editor is vi(1), the standard full-screen editor accompanying all UNIX systems. Use vi to create and modify any text file. During this discussion, since editing mostly occurs on the screen, all examples appear in an enclosed fifty-column, fifteen-line screen. The cursor's location on this screen is indicated by a single underscore (_).

To start vi and edit the new file file1, use the following command. Your home directory is the current directory for this example:

```
$ vi file1 ↵
```

The screen clears and the following appears:

```
_
~
~
~
~
~
~
~
~
~
~
~
~
~
"file1" [New file]
```

If your terminal and shell are not properly configured, vi may respond with:

```
unknown: Unknown terminal type
I don't know what kind of terminal you are on - all I have is "unknown"
[Using open mode]
"file1" [New file]

_
```

If you receive these messages, your *TERM* shell variable is not properly set. You should exit vi by typing :q! and then pressing ENTER. To correct the problem, either correct the value assigned to the *TERM* variable (as discussed in Chapter 3) or ask your system administrator for assistance.

NOTE: Just in case, to exit vi without saving what you have done, press the ESC key followed by :q! and then press RETURN. To exit but save what you have done, press the ESC key followed by :wq! and then press RETURN.

Once vi displays the full-screen with tildes in column 1 of each line, continue with the next section.

EDITING MODES

Vi has two operating modes: text entry mode and command mode. The normal mode for vi operation is command mode. Text entry mode is entered from command mode when you attempt to insert or replace text. To exit text entry mode, thus returning to command mode, press the ESC key.

On some terminals, notably the Digital Equipment VT100, the ESC key is available only from one of the function keys and only when the terminal has been configured to operate in this manner. If your terminal does not have an ESC key, you can press CTRL-[instead.

INSERTING TEXT

On the vi screen, notice that the first character of each line is a tilde (~). The tilde indicates that no text is present in that line. Once you insert a character into a line, the tilde disappears.

Time to insert some text into the file. To insert text using vi, press the i key and enter the following text as shown (complete with errors):

```
The following text is an example of how to enter ⏎
information in to a text file.  An completion of ⏎
```

```
this exercise, the esc key are pressed.⏎
⏎
More text complicates the file.  Not that we need ⏎
more compilcations, but it also increases the ⏎
number of exmpales that can be derived from one ⏎
block of text. ⏎
```

While entering this text, you may accidentally create more errors than are already present. Don't worry about it. You'll learn how to correct them in the next several sections.

While entering a line of text, you may use the BACKSPACE key to back up and correct an error. Once you complete a line by pressing the ENTER key, you cannot use the BACKSPACE key to go back; however, additional errors in the text are not fatal to the exercise. Use the BACKSPACE key to correct what you type when you are in text entry mode.

After you have entered the text, press the ESC key to leave text entry mode and return to command mode. The vi screen should look like this:

```
   The following text is an example of how to enter
   information in to a text file.  An completion of
   this exercise, the esc key are pressed.

   More text complicates the file.  Not that we need
   more compilcations, but it also increases the
   number of exmpales that can be derived from one
   block of text.
   _
   ~
   ~
   ~
   ~
   ~
   "file1" [New file]
```

Notice that the status line has not changed. It continues to display the name of the file and indicates that the file is new. Once a message is displayed on the status line, it stays until you either scroll text past the bottom or execute a command that produces a new status message. After a while you'll get used to it.

MOVING THE CURSOR

Before you can correct errors in the text, you need to know how to move the cursor. Before you can move your cursor with any key other than the BACKSPACE key, vi must be in command mode. Press ESC to ensure that vi is in command mode.

If your terminal is equipped with cursor movement keys (usually identified by the arrows ← , → , ↓ , and ↑), you may use these keys to move the cursor—in the direction indicated by the arrow—to any character in the text. If your terminal does not have cursor keys or they do not work, you may use the following keys to perform the same movements:

h — Move left one character.
j — Move down one line.
k — Move up one line.
l — Move right one character.

Experiment for a moment with cursor movement. Move the cursor to the end of any line. Notice that vi beeps when you attempt to move past the end of the line. It also will beep if you attempt to move to the left of the first character of any line, above the first line in the file, or below the last line in the file.

To move the cursor in any direction a certain number of times, you may precede any cursor movement key by a number. For example, to move up three lines, type 3k (or 3 ↑).

Cursor jumps also are provided with a single keystroke:

0 — (zero) Move to the beginning of the current line.
$ — Move to the last character of the current line.
G — Move to the first character of the file's last line.

Other techniques for cursor movement are discussed later in this chapter.

ADDING TEXT

Since you cannot move the cursor to the right of the last character in any line, how do you append information?

To append text, use either a (append after the character at the current cursor position) or A (append to the end of the current line). Use the i command to insert text before the character at the cursor position; I inserts text before the first character in the line (similar to using 0i).

For example, move the cursor to any spot in the last line and press A. The cursor moves to the space immediately after the period, and you are now in text entry mode. Now type two spaces and the phrase *Or something*. Press ESC to leave text entry mode. Your screen now looks like this:

```
    The following text is an example of how to enter
    information in to a text file.  An completion of
    this exercise, the esc key are pressed.

    More text complicates the file.  Not that we need
    more compilcations, but it also increases the
    number of exmpales that can be derived from one
    block of text.  Or something.

    ~
    ~
    ~
    ~
    ~
    "file1" [New file]
```

The command to insert a line after the current line is o (lowercase O). Use uppercase 0 to insert a line before the current line. For example, press 0 right now and the screen changes as follows:

```
    The following text is an example of how to enter
    information in to a text file.  An completion of
    this exercise, the esc key are pressed.

    More text complicates the file.  Not that we need
    more compilcations, but it also increases the
    number of exmpales that can be derived from one

    _
    block of text.  Or something.

    ~
    ~
    ~
    ~
    "file1" [New file]
```

Both 0 and o place vi in text entry mode. After inserting a line, enter text and press ESC to finish. Right now, more text is not needed in the file, so just press ESC to conclude this section.

SOME SIMPLE WAYS TO EDIT THE TEXT

Let's correct a few of the errors in the text. Move the cursor to the first error (*in to* should be changed to *into*):

```
The following text is an example of how to enter
information in_to a text file.  An completion of
this exercise, the esc key are pressed.

More text complicates the file.  Not that we need
more compilcations, but it also increases the
number of exmpales that can be derived from one

block of text.  Or something.

~
~
~
~
"file1" [New file]
```

To remove the extra space, press x. The x command deletes a single character at the cursor location. As with the cursor movement keys, you may precede x by a number to delete more than one character. For example, 4x deletes four characters beginning at the cursor.

Now move to the word *esc*. Instead of *esc*, this word should read *ESC*. Move the cursor to the *e* in *esc* and press the tilde key. This key automatically changes uppercase letters to lowercase and vice versa and then moves the cursor one character to the right. You also may precede this command with a number to convert more than one character. Type 2~. The text now looks like this:

```
The following text is an example of how to enter
information into a text file.  An completion of
this exercise, the ESC_key are pressed.
```

(continued)

```
   More text complicates the file.  Not that we need
   more compilcations, but it also increases the
   number of exmpales that can be derived from one

   block of text.  Or something.

   ~
   ~
   ~
   ~
   "file" [New file]
```

Now move back to the word *An*. This word should read *On*. To change a
single character, use the command r (replace character). Press r and then type
O. The screen should look like this:

```
   The following text is an example of how to enter
   information into a text file.  On completion of
   this exercise, the ESC key are pressed.

   More text complicates the file.  Not that we need
   more compilcations, but it also increases the
   number of exmpales that can be derived from one

   block of text.  Or something.

   ~
   ~
   ~
   ~
   "file1" [New file]
```

Now move the cursor to the first i in *compilcations* (in the sixth line). The
characters *il* should be changed to *li*. With vi, the easiest way to make this
change is to type xp. The x command deletes a single letter, the *i*. The command p (put) copies the last deleted item back into the text immediately
after the cursor.

Now move the cursor down to the word *exmpales* in the seventh line. One
way to correct the spelling of this word to examples is to use x, move the
cursor, and use p. Another way is to use the command R (overwrite) to

replace the three letters with the correct three letters.

Move the cursor to the *m* in *exmpales* and press R. Type *amp*. Notice that vi overwrites the characters. Since you are in text entry mode, press ESC. The screen should now look like this:

```
The following text is an example of how to enter
information into a text file.  On completion of
this exercise, the ESC key are pressed.

More text complicates the file.  Not that we need
more complications, but it also increases the
number of examples that can be derived from one


block of text.  Or something.


~
~
~
~
"file1" [New file]
```

Let's add one more line of text. Move the cursor to the last line and insert the text *The End*, using the i command. Press ESC and your screen now appears as follows:

```
The following text is an example of how to enter
information into a text file.  On completion of
this exercise, the ESC key are pressed.

More text complicates the file.  Not that we need
more complications, but it also increases the
number of examples that can be derived from one

block of text.  Or something.
The End.

~

~

~

~
"file1" [New file]
```

Since the last two lines are short, let's join them together. Move your cursor anywhere in the next to last line and press J (for join):

```
       The following text is an example of how to enter
       information into a text file.  On completion of
       this exercise, the ESC key are pressed.

       More text complicates the file.  Not that we need
       more complications, but it also increases the
       number of examples that can be derived from one

       block of text.  Or something._ The End.
       ~
       ~
       ~
       ~
       ~
    "file1" [New file]
```

The extra space between the end of *Or something.* and the beginning of *The End.* was added by vi, which understands the concept of sentences. For more about sentences, see "Complex Cursor Movement within Vi" after the next section. Note that the cursor moved to the first character of the joined text and that the file shrank by one line.

A QUICK REVIEW

This is the halfway point in this chapter. It's time for a quick break. Table 4-1 provides a quick review of the vi commands you have learned.

Table 4-1. Quick Review

Cursor Keys and Commands	
Key/Command	**Cursor Movement**
←, →, ↓, ↑	Left, right, down, up, respectively
h, j, k, l	Left, down, up, right, respectively; can be preceded by a number to cause the cursor to move more than one character

Table 4-1. Quick Review (continued)

Cursors Keys and Commands (continued)	
Key/Command	**Cursor Movement**
0	(Zero) To the beginning of the current line
$	To the end of the current line
G	To the end of the file
Edit Commands	
Command	**vi Function**
i	Enter text entry mode (insert text at the current cursor position).
I	Move to the first character in the current line and enter text entry mode.
a	Append text (enter text entry mode) after the current cursor position.
A	Append text (enter text entry mode) at the end of the current line.
o, O	Insert a blank line after/before the current line (enter text entry mode at the beginning of the new line).
x	Delete the character at the cursor position; may be preceded by a number to delete multiple characters.
xp	Swap the current character with the character immediately following it (this command is really the x (delete) command followed by the p (put) command).
~	Change the case of the character at the cursor position; may be preceded by a number to change multiple characters.

Table 4-1. Quick Review (continued)

Edit Commands (continued)	
Command	**vi Function**
r	Replace a single character; may be preceded by a number to change multiple characters.
R	Replace a set of characters (stay in text entry mode and replace characters until ESC is pressed).
J	Join the current line with the following line.
ESC	Use the ESC key to leave text entry mode.
:q!	Exit without saving changes to the current file.
:wq!	Save the changes to the current file and exit the editor.

COMPLEX CURSOR MOVEMENT WITHIN VI

In vi, you have numerous ways to move the cursor through your document besides the ones discussed earlier. This section describes three additional ways.

vi Objects

Vi understands the concept of *objects* within your file. An object may be a word, a sentence, or a paragraph.

A word is defined as a consecutive group of letters and numbers; the end of a word is delimited by a space, punctuation, a symbol, or the end of a line. A sentence is a group of characters ending in a period, exclamation point, or question mark, followed by either the end of a line or by two spaces; sentences may contain any number of consecutive lines. A paragraph is a group of sentences that ends with either at least one blank line or the end of the file.

Some of the commands used to perform object-based cursor movement include the following:

w — Move to the first character of the next word.

b — Move back to the first character of either the current word or the previous word.

e — Move forward to the last character of either the current or the next word.

) — Move to the beginning of the next sentence.

(— Move back to the beginning of either the current sentence or the previous sentence.

} — Move to the beginning of the next paragraph.

{ — Move back to the beginning of either the current paragraph or the previous paragraph.

In other words:

❏ If the cursor is in the middle of a word, b moves the cursor to the first character of that word.

❏ If the cursor is at the beginning of a word, b moves the cursor to the beginning of the previous word.

Vi uses the same logic for the other object-based movement commands. You may precede each of these commands with a number, causing vi to perform a longer cursor move. For example, move your cursor to the letter *p* in the word *examples*:

```
The following text is an example of how to enter
information into a text file.  On completion of
this exercise, the ESC key are pressed.

More text complicates the file.  Not that we need
more complications, but it also increases the
number of examples that can be derived from one

block of text.  Or something.  The End.
~

~
```

(continued)

```
~
~
~
"file1" [New file]
```

To move to the end of the word *that*, type `2e`. To move to the beginning of the paragraph, type `{`. Your screen now looks like this:

```
The following text is an example of how to enter
information into a text file.  On completion of
this exercise, the ESC key are pressed.

More text complicates the file.  Not that we need
more complications, but it also increases the
number of examples that can be derived from one

block of text.  Or something.  The End.
~
~
~
~
~
"file1" [New file]
```

To move back two words, type `2b`. The cursor is now at the beginning of the word *pressed*.

Two concepts to note:

1. Unlike the other cursor movement commands discussed thus far, object-based cursor movement commands do not stop at the end or beginning of a line.

2. Punctuation is a word in `vi`, and `vi` counts it in all word-based cursor movement commands.

Searching

The cursor movement commands discussed so far are satisfactory if you know exactly where in the file you need to edit; however, most of the time you don't. So, `vi` lets you search for text within the file via the commands / (search forward) and ? (search backward).

Continuing with the example file you've been editing, press ↑ to move to the beginning of the file. Let's search for the string *of*. Press / to initiate the search command. Your screen now looks like this:

```
The following text is an example of how to enter
information into a text file.  On completion of
this exercise, the ESC key are pressed.

More text complicates the file.  Not that we need
more complications, but it also increases the
number of examples that can be derived from one

block of text.  Or something.  The End.
~
~
~
~
~
/_
```

The / you entered is echoed on the status line and the cursor is next to it. Now type *of*. These characters are also echoed; if you make a mistake, use BACKSPACE to correct the error. Once you have typed *of*, press ENTER. The cursor jumps to the first occurrence of *of*:

```
The following text is an example of how to enter
information into a text file.  On completion of
this exercise, the ESC key are pressed.

More text complicates the file.  Not that we need
more complications, but it also increases the
number of examples that can be derived from one

block of text.  Or something.  The End.
~
~
~
~
~
/of
```

To repeat this search, press / and then ENTER. Now your screen looks like:

```
    The following text is an example of how to enter
    information into a text file.  On completion of
    this exercise, the ESC key are pressed.

    More text complicates the file.  Not that we need
    more complications, but it also increases the
    number of examples that can be derived from one

    block of text.  Or something.  The End.
    ~
    ~
    ~
    ~
    ~
    /
```

To jump to the previous occurrence of *of*, press ? and then press ENTER. Notice on your screen that the question mark now appears on the status line. To search for the previous occurrence of *a*, enter the command ?a and press ENTER.

When the search reaches the top or bottom of the file, it continues from the other end of the file. In other words, the search is circular. If the search string is not matched, the message "Not found" is displayed on the status line.

The command n repeats the last search in the same direction specified for the search; N repeats the last search in the opposite direction. After all the jumps in the last few paragraphs, your screen should appear like this:

```
    The following text is an example of how to enter
    information into a text file.  On completion of
    this exercise, the ESC key are pressed.

    More text complicates the file.  Not that we need
    more complications, but it also increases the
    number of examples that can be derived from one

                                        (continued)
```

```
block of text.  Or something.  The End.
~
~
~
~
~
?a
```

To move to the previous *a*, press n; the cursor moves to the *a* in *an*. Press n again. The screen now looks like this:

```
The following text is an example of how to enter
information into a text file.  On completion of
this exercise, the ESC key are pressed.

More text complicates the file.  Not that we need
more complications, but it also increases the
number of examples that can be derived from one

block of text.  Or something.  The End.
~
~
~
~
~
?a
```

To go back to the *a* in *an*, press N. N does not change the direction of the search; it causes a one-time search in the opposite direction. Pressing n again moves the cursor back to the word *can* in the seventh line of the document.

Page by Page

Vi also provides commands for paging through the file. To move down one screen, press CTRL-F; to move up one screen, press CTRL-B. Preceding these commands by a number specifies the number of screens to move. Unless you are working with large files, these commands aren't very useful.

To move up half a screen, press CTRL-U; to move down one-half screen, press CTRL-D. To adjust the number of lines the cursor moves for either of these commands, enter the number of lines before entering the command. For example, if you want to move the cursor up only five lines with CTRL-

U, type 5^U; subsequent uses of CTRL-U move the cursor up five lines (until you change the number of lines again); subsequent uses of CTRL-D move the cursor down five lines.

MORE EDITING WITHIN VI

The cursor movement commands discussed so far also provide a way to edit blocks of text larger than a single character. The three main commands this section describes are c (change), d (delete), and y (yank).

The commands c, d, and y require you to specify how much you want to change, delete, or yank, respectively. For example, to delete a single word, the command is dw; to change two words use 2cw. The cursor movement commands G, $, 0, b, w,), (, }, and { are often used with these commands. You may also use the search commands with these edit commands; for example, to delete everything between the cursor and the next occurrence of the word *World*, use the command d/World.

Move your cursor to the last line, as shown:

```
    The following text is an example of how to enter
    information into a text file.  On completion of
    this exercise, the ESC key are pressed.

    More text complicates the file.  Not that we need
    more complications, but it also increases the
    number of examples that can be derived from one

    block of text._ Or something.  The End.
    ~
    ~
    ~
    ~
    ~
```

To delete everything from the cursor to the end of the line, type d$. Notice that the cursor moves one space to the left; the delete command always starts from the cursor position. Another way to perform the d$ command is to press a single D.

The dd command deletes a single line. You may specify a number before the command to delete more than one line. Move the cursor up one line and type dd:

```
The following text is an example of how to enter
information into a text file.  On completion of
this exercise, the ESC key are pressed.

More text complicates the file.  Not that we need
more complications, but it also increases the
number of examples that can be derived from one
block of text.
~
  ~
  ~
  ~
  ~
  ~
```

The c command is similar to R in that it permits you to change text. With c, however, you must specify at the start how much of the original text to change. The new text does not need to be the same length as the text it replaced, as it must when you use R.

For example, the word *are* in the third line of the text should be *is*. Move the cursor to the *a* in *are* and type cw to change the word. Notice that a $ appears on the last character of the word; this sign marks the end of the original text to change. Now type *is*. Since you are in text entry mode, press ESC to complete the change. The line is shortened by one character because *is* is one character shorter than *are*. The screen now looks like this:

```
The following text is an example of how to enter
information into a text file.  On completion of
this exercise, the ESC key is pressed.

More text complicates the file.  Not that we need
more complications, but it also increases the
number of examples that can be derived from one
block of text.
~
  ~
```

(continued)

```
~
~
~
~
```

If you make a mistake, you can undo the most recent edit with the u command. To change *is* back to *are*, press u; this change becomes your last edit. Now press u again to reverse the edit and change *are* back to *is*. Having fun yet?

The u command reverses only the last insertion, deletion, change, replacement, or put; it does not reverse a search. You can undo a series of consecutive changes made to a single line with U.

Use the put command p to recover the most recent deletion. For example, to reverse the two paragraphs in the file, move the cursor to the first row and type 4dd. Now move the cursor to the bottom row and press p. Your file now appears like this:

```
More text complicates the file.  Not that we need
more complications, but it also increases the
number of examples that can be derived from one
block of text.
The following text is an example of how to enter
information into a text file.  On completion of
this exercise, the ESC key is pressed.
~
~
~
~
~
~
~
```

Pressing u undoes the p (put) command and not the deletion, since p was the last edit command. You can press p again to place another copy of this paragraph in the file. You may also use P to place a copy of the paragraph in the file before the cursor position.

The d and p commands let you move blocks of text. To copy blocks of text, vi provides the y (yank or copy) command. Move to the block of text you want to copy and yank the object as you would have deleted it (using either y and a cursor movement key or yy to yank the whole line). Notice that the line does not disappear. If the number of lines yanked is greater than four, a message telling you how many lines have been yanked appears on the status line.

By the way, just as dd deletes a line and yy copies a line, cc permits you to change an entire line regardless of where in the line the cursor is positioned.

Now put the cursor where you wish to place a copy of the object you just yanked. Press either p (put after the cursor) or P (put before the cursor).

Spend some time now practicing the commands discussed in this section.

REPEATING AN EDIT

Not only does vi remember the last edit sequence for the u command, you can also repeat this sequence at another location with the period (.) command. For example, search for the letters *the* in the file (using the / command). Now use either the c or R command to change this word to *any*.

To repeat the search and replacement, press n and then press the period. The edit sequence that is remembered is the change, not the search; moving the cursor anywhere in the file and pressing the period repeats the change irrespective of the text being replaced.

SAVING YOUR WORK AND EXITING VI

So far I have not discussed vi's origins. Vi is actually an extension to the ex(1) line-oriented editor also provided with UNIX. You may execute ex commands from vi command mode by preceding the command with a colon. For example, to move to line 4 in the file, type :4 and then press ENTER.

These commands are called *colon commands*. Chapter 8 discusses the importance of the colon commands. For now, you need them to save the changes made to a file and to exit vi.

While you have been editing with vi, you have not been modifying the contents of the file you requested, but an internal work area that vi maintains. Throughout this book, if no distinction needs to be made, the file and the work area are used synonymously.

To retain the changes you have made to the work area, you must save them to a file. To save your work, type :w. Notice that what you typed appears on the status line:

```
    More text complicates the file.  Not that we need
    more complications, but it also increases the
    number of examples that can be derived from one
    block of text.
    The following text is an example of how to enter
    information into a text file.  On completion of
    this exercise, the ESC key is pressed.
    ~
    ~
    ~
    ~
    ~
    ~
    ~
    :w_
```

Press ENTER. The status line changes to indicate what you have saved:

```
    More text complicates the file.  Not that we need
    more complications, but it also increases the
    number of examples that can be derived from one
    block of text.
    The following text is an example of how to enter
    information into a text file.  On completion of
    this exercise, the ESC key is pressed.
    ~
    ~
    ~
    ~
    ~
    ~
    ~
    "file1" [New file] 9 lines 295 characters
```

To leave vi, type :q and press ENTER. If you try to leave vi without saving your most recent changes, vi will display this message on the status line:

```
No write since last change (:quit! overrides).
```

To exit vi without saving your changes, type :q! and press ENTER.

To save your work under a filename that differs from the one specified when you started vi, type :w, a space, the new filename, and then press ENTER. For example, to save your current work area as ft1, type :w ft1 and press ENTER.

You may combine the :w and :q commands as :wq. Another way to perform :wq is ZZ. You do not need to press ENTER to execute ZZ.

If you want to edit another file while you are still within vi, type :e, a space, the name of the new file to edit, and then press ENTER (for example, :e .profile). The contents of the new file are placed into the vi work area, and the previous contents of the work area are lost. If you have not saved the most recent changes to the work area, vi will instruct you either to save the work area first or to use :e! instead of :e.

GOT ALL THAT?

Refer to Table 4-2 for a quick review of everything you've learned in this chapter. The items from the earlier review are repeated for completeness.

Table 4-2. Chapter Review

Cursor Movement Keys	
Key/Command	**Cursor Movement**
←, →, ↓,↑	Left, right, down, up, respectively
h, j, k, l	Left, down, up, right, respectively; can be preceded by a number to cause the cursor to move more than one character
0	(Zero) To the beginning of the current line
$	To the end of the line
G	To the end of the file
w	To the first character of the next word

Table 4-2. Chapter Review (continued)

Cursor Movement Keys (continued)	
Key/Command	**Cursor Movement**
b	Back to the first character of a word
e	Forward to the last character of a word
)	To the beginning of the next sentence
(	Back to the beginning of a sentence
}	To the beginning of the next paragraph
{	Back to the beginning of a paragraph
^F	Down one screen
^B	Up one screen
^U	Up half a screen; precede with a number to change the number of lines in a half-screen
^D	Down half a screen; precede with a number to change the number of lines in a half-screen
:#	To line # in the file
Search Commands	
Command	**Function**
/string	Search forward through the file for the string.
?string	Search backward through the file for the string.
n	Repeat the search in the same direction.
N	Repeat the search in the opposite direction.

Table 4-2. Chapter Review (continued)

Editing Commands	
Command	**Operation**
i	Enter text entry mode (insert text at the cursor).
I	Move to the first character in the current line and enter text entry mode.
a	Append text (enter text entry mode) after the cursor.
A	Append text (enter text entry mode) at the end of the current line.
o, O	Insert a blank line after/before the current line (enter text entry mode at the beginning of the new line).
x	Delete the character at the cursor; may be preceded by a number to delete multiple characters.
c*obj*	Change text between the cursor and the character defined by the object-based cursor movement *obj*. For example, c$ changes all characters between the cursor and the end of the current line and places you in text entry mode.
d*obj*	Delete text between the cursor and the character defined by the object-based cursor movement command *obj*. For example, d} deletes all characters between the cursor and the end of the paragraph. Use p or P to put the text back into the file at another location.
dd	Delete the current line. Precede with a number to delete multiple lines. Use p or P to put the text back into the file at another location.

Table 4-2. Chapter Review (continued)

Editing Commands (continued)	
Command	**Operation**
y*obj*	Yank (copy) the text between the cursor and the object-based cursor movement command *obj*. For example, y) yanks all characters between the cursor and the end of the sentence. Use p or P to place this text in another location.
p, P	Put the characters most recently deleted or yanked back into the file either before (p) or after (P) the cursor position.
r	Replace a single character; may be preceded by a number to change more than one character.
R	Replace a set of characters (stay in text entry mode and replace characters until ESC is pressed).
~	Change the case of the character at the cursor; may be preceded by a number to change multiple characters.
u, U	Undo the most recent single change (u) or the most recent consecutive changes (U).
.	Repeat the most recent edit.
J	Join the current line with the following line.
ESC	Just a reminder: Use the ESC key to leave text entry mode.
ZZ	Save changes and exit the file. Same as :wq!
:q, :q!	Exit vi without saving changes to the current file.

Table 4-2. Chapter Review (continued)

Editing Commands (continued)	
Command	**Operation**
`:wq`, `:wq!`	Save the changes to the file and exit the editor.
`:e`, `:e!`	Edit another file without leaving the editor.

CAN THIS BE THE END?

Nah. But you have completed Part I of this book. You now know enough about UNIX to log in, create files, run programs, edit files, and determine the status of the system. Not bad for a few hours' work.

Okay, take five. Let's go get something to eat.

Part II

Getting to Know UNIX

To take full advantage of UNIX, you need to learn more about your shell and how to configure it. You also need to learn about some of the utilities provided with UNIX.

Chapter 5 shows you how to configure and use your shell environment. Chapter 6 introduces you to shell programming and shows you how to use shell programming to improve your shell environment. Chapter 7 discusses some useful utilities.

After this part of the book, you will know so much about UNIX that your peers will be jealous and want to get their own copy of this book.

Okay by me.

Chapter 5

Configuring and Using
Your Shell

Chapter 3 discussed the concept of the UNIX shell and showed you how to determine which shell you are using. This chapter discusses how to configure and use your shell. It is divided into three parts: one discusses the Bourne shell, one discusses the C shell, and one very briefly discusses the Korn shell.

Regardless of which shell you choose as your login shell, you should review all of the information provided in this chapter.

A QUICK REVIEW BEFORE YOU START

Since much of this chapter indirectly refers to the shell variable discussion in Chapter 3, here's a quick review of the shell variables already discussed:

HOME—Your home directory; the directory from which you start when you log in to your account.

SHELL—The location of your shell program (for example, /bin/csh).

PATH—Like DOS, this variable contains a list of directories searched for each program you execute.

LOGNAME—Your login account name.

TERM—The variable defining the type of terminal you are using.

TZ—The current time zone specification.

EDITOR—The name of your editor program (for example, /usr/bin/vi).

THE BOURNE SHELL

When you log in with the Bourne shell, the following shell scripts (similar to the concept of DOS batch files) are automatically executed:

/etc/profile—The systemwide Bourne shell command file, which contains the commands that the system administrator wants all users to execute when logging in.

$HOME/.profile—The user-specific Bourne shell command file, which contains the commands you want to execute each time you log in. You are responsible for creating and maintaining this file; by the end of this section, you will know how.

When you start a Bourne shell, but before /etc/profile runs, the shell automatically assigns a value to the *LOGNAME* variable.

Usually /etc/profile contains commands to set the shell variables *PATH*, *TZ*, *TERM*, and *SHELL*. Your .profile file should adjust the *PATH* variable, assign a value to the *EDITOR* variable, automatically read your electronic mail when you log in, and set other Bourne shell-specific shell variables.

To change the prompt displayed by the shell (in this book the prompt is represented by $), assign a new value to the shell variable *PS1*. For example:

```
$ PS1="Shell> "  ↵
Shell> _
```

Now your shell prompt is Shell>. To change your shell prompt back to the dollar sign:

```
Shell> PS1="$ "  ↵
$ _
```

To set your *PATH* variable, specify a list of directories separated by a colon. For example, to set your search path to include /bin, /usr/bin, /usr/local/bin, the current directory, your home directory, and /usr/lib, enter the following:

```
$ PATH=/bin:/usr/bin:/usr/local/bin:.:$HOME:/usr/lib  ↵
```

As discussed in Chapter 3, shell variables control not only the operation of the shell but also the operation of certain UNIX utilities. For example, vi uses the *TERM* variable to determine how to control your terminal.

The value assigned to a shell variable may either be available only to the shell itself or provided to (inherited by) any program executed from the shell. To cause a variable's value to be inherited, you must *export* the variable. Exported variables are also called *environment variables*; nonexported variables are called *local variables*.

The following example demonstrates the effect of export on shell variables:

```
$ PS1="Shell> " ⏎
Shell> _
```

So far, the variable *PS1* has been set to Shell>. To export this variable, use:

```
Shell> export PS1 ⏎
Shell> _
```

As you can see, exporting a variable does not change its appearance. Now, let's start another shell:

```
Shell> /bin/sh ⏎
Shell> _
```

The value for *PS1* in this shell was inherited from the previous shell. If we had run a program like vi instead of a shell, the effect would have been the same; the value for *PS1* would be Shell>.

Unless you export the variable, subsequent programs do not receive the most recent value for the variable. Let's prove it by changing the value for the variable, not exporting it within this shell and then running another shell:

```
Shell> PS1="Shell2: " ⏎
Shell2: /bin/sh ⏎
Shell> _
```

Although *PS1* was set to Shell2: in the previous shell, the variable was not exported in the shell, so the new value was not inherited. A variable need only be exported once in a particular shell to cause any subsequent shell (or program) to receive the variable's current value.

To show that the previous shell's value has not been changed:

```
Shell> exit ⏎
Shell2: _ ⏎
```

The value for *PS1* has not changed in the second shell, but what about the initial shell?

```
Shell2: exit
Shell> _
```

You should assign and export *PS1* in your `.profile` file.

More About Environment Variables

When a program starts, it receives a list containing the defined environment variables and their current values. Variables that have not been exported do not appear in this list. You can read more about this list in the manual entry for `environ`(5).

Many UNIX commands and utilities use the variables *TERM, TZ, SHELL*, and *EDITOR*. Values are usually assigned to the first three variables in `/etc/profile`, although you may assign new values in your `.profile`. *EDITOR*'s value is usually initialized in your `.profile`.

The value for *TERM* is a string identifying the type of terminal you are using (for example, vt220).

All system time programs, such as `date`(1), use the *TZ* variable to choose the time zone for the time to display. For example, if you are using your UNIX system in Boston, your time zone is Eastern, so set your *TZ* variable to EST5EDT. See `environ`(5) for a discussion of the format for this value.

Essentially, the first three *TZ* characters are the time zone abbreviation during the winter; the digit specifies the number of hours west of Greenwich mean time (GMT) your time zone is located (Eastern time zone is five hours west of GMT), and the final three characters indicate not only that your location has a daylight saving time period, but the abbreviation for this period. In most of Arizona, which does not have daylight saving time, set *TZ* to MST7.

Programs such as `vi` (see Chapter 8) that may start a new shell for you use the *SHELL* variable to select which shell to run. The value for this variable is the program name of your login shell (for example, `/bin/sh`).

Programs such as `mailx` (see Chapter 7) that need a text editor use the *EDITOR* variable. You should assign the *EDITOR* variable in your `.profile` to the complete file path to the editor you use. For example, if you use `vi`, set *EDITOR* to `/usr/bin/vi` and not merely `vi`, since some programs may not use your search path to locate programs.

Once you have assigned values to them, always export these variables. To view the values for all environment variables, use the command `env`:

```
Shell> env ←
HOME=/users/amf
LOGNAME=amf
MAIL=/usr/spool/mail/amf
PS1=Shell>
PATH=/bin:/usr/bin:/etc:/usr/lib:/usr/local/bin:/usr/contrib/bin
SHELL=/bin/sh
TERM=ansi
TZ=EST5EDT
Shell> _
```

To view all variables that are local to the current shell, use the command set with no arguments:

```
Shell> set ←
HOME=/users/amf
IFS=

LOGNAME=amf
MAIL=/usr/spool/mail/amf
PATH=/bin:/usr/bin:/etc:/usr/lib:/usr/local/bin:/usr/contrib/bin
PS1=Shell>
PS2=>
SHELL=/bin/sh
TERM=ansi
TZ=EST5EDT
Shell> _
```

Notice that many variables in the set listing are the same as those in env. Remember: Exported variables resemble local variables in the current shell, but only the values for exported variables are available to other programs you execute.

To view a single variable, use echo(1):

```
Shell> echo $SHELL ←
/bin/sh
Shell> _
```

REMINDER: The $ is required to reference a shell variable's value.

Redirecting stderr

Chapter 3 did not discuss redirection of standard error (stderr) because each shell performs this task differently. In the Bourne shell, stderr can be redirected either to stdout's destination or to another location.

Remember from Chapter 3 that each UNIX process automatically opens stdin, stdout, and stderr. These files are opened in exactly that order and automatically receive file descriptors 0, 1, and 2, respectively. UNIX uses a file descriptor to keep track of each open file. When you open a file, the operating system assigns it a file descriptor; the descriptor is then used for all future operations, like reading or writing.

Using these file descriptors, you can redirect any standard file. For example, to redirect stdout and stderr from the program `cmnd` to the same file, do the following:

```
$ cmnd 1>file 2>&1 ⏎
```

The `1>file` notation causes the shell to route output from stdout to `file` (the same as, but more explicit than, the notation `>file`). The notation `2>&1` causes the shell to route output from stderr to the same location as stdout. The ampersand precedes the stdout descriptor to distinguish the file descriptor 1 (stdout) from the file named 1.

The shell evaluates redirections left to right on the command line. Suppose you change the above command to:

```
$ cmnd 2>&1 1>file ⏎
```

Processed left to right, stderr is redirected to the location for stdout, currently the terminal. Then stdout is redirected to `file`; stderr remains redirected to the terminal.

Note that the command

```
$ cmnd 1>file 2>&1 ⏎
```

is different from

```
$ cmnd 1>file 2>file ⏎
```

The first command redirects stderr to stdout, which then redirects the output to `file`. In the second command, stdout and stderr each have `file` open and write to the file independently, never knowing that another source is placing information in the file; information from stdout will overwrite information from stderr and vice versa.

In general, programs route only error and warning messages to stderr. If you are not interested in this information, redirect stderr to the device file /dev/null, the UNIX bit bucket:

```
$ cmnd 2>/dev/null ⏎
```

You can also pipe stderr to the same location as stdout:

```
$ command1 2>&1 | lp ⏎
```

This redirects stderr to stdout, and all output from stdout is piped to lp.

So How Do You Create a .profile File?

The .profile file is a Bourne shell script file. A shell script file is similar to a DOS batch (.BAT) file; it contains commands that you want to execute as a set. An example of a DOS batch file is AUTOEXEC.BAT, which runs when a DOS system starts. The uses for .profile are similar to the uses for AUTOEXEC.BAT: to run a set of commands that configure your environment in a manner that pleases you.

You can use vi to create .profile. Here is an example .profile file. The line numbers are used only to make it easier to describe the file's contents; do not enter the line numbers into your .profile.

```
1
2  #
3  # This is my start-up script
4  #
5  TERM=ansi
6  SHELL=/bin/sh
7  PATH=$PATH:/usr/games/bin:$HOME/project/bin
8  EDITOR=/usr/bin/vi
9  PS1="BSH> "
10
11 export TERM SHELL PATH EDITOR PS1
12
13 echo "Welcome. Today's date is `date`"
```

The first character of the first line of a .profile file (and any Bourne shell script file) should not be a #. This character indicates that the following characters are commentary and are not interpreted by the shell. Blank lines in a shell script are also considered comment lines.

Lines 2 through 4 are comments.

Lines 5 through 9 assign new values to the shell variables *TERM*, *SHELL*, *PATH*, *EDITOR*, and *PS1*. Line 11 exports these variables so that other programs can use their values.

When line 13 executes, a message like this is displayed on your terminal:

```
Welcome. Today's date is Sat Jul 21 13:21:20 1990
```

The Bourne shell provides other commands and features that you can use with `.profile` or any Bourne shell script (see Chapters 6 and 9).

THE C SHELL

As you may have guessed from the previous section, the Bourne shell environment is as limited as the user environment DOS provides. When possible, you should not use the Bourne shell as your login shell; use either the C shell or the Korn shell. By the end of this chapter, you will understand why.

NOTE: The C shell did not originate as part of UNIX System V; it was adapted from work performed at the University of California at Berkeley. Therefore, some UNIX implementations provide C shell features not described in this chapter. If you find a problem, consult the `csh(1)` entry in your *UNIX Reference Manual*.

When you log in to the C shell, these scripts automatically execute:

`$HOME/.cshrc` — A C shell command file that you create and maintain and that every C shell you start executes prior to any other processing performed by the shell. If the shell is your login shell, `$HOME/.login` executes immediately following the completion of all commands in this file.

`$HOME/.login` — Another C shell command file that you create and maintain and that executes only when a C shell is started as your login shell. When you log in, these commands execute immediately after the commands in `$HOME/.cshrc` are processed.

In addition, a few UNIX systems provide a systemwide login script containing commands that the administrator wants all C shell users to execute when logging in. Each system uses a different name for this file, but if present, this file is found in the `/etc` directory. The commands in this file are executed before `.cshrc`.

If your system has a systemwide login script, it performs these tasks: setting a good `stty` to control all terminals; setting values for the environment variables *SHELL, PATH, TERM, TZ,* and *EDITOR*; and reporting if a user has received new electronic mail. If your system has no such script, these tasks should be included in your `$HOME/.login`.

Both `.cshrc` and `.login` are shell script files. Creating these files is similar to creating `.profile` (which is used only by the Bourne shell). The commands are slightly different, but the intent is the same.

The `.cshrc` script should define any shell variables used to control the shell's operation (for example, the *history* variable, described below). Use the `.cshrc` file to also specify any *aliases*, or synonyms, for certain commands; see below.

The `.login` script should include commands to define any environment variables and to perform tasks that you want to do only when you log in, such as read your electronic mail.

Setting an environment variable in the C shell is different from doing it in the Bourne shell. To set a C shell environment variable, you need only one command: `setenv`. For example, to set your *TERM* variable to vt100, enter:

```
$ setenv TERM vt100 ⏎
```

Many of the environment variables used with the C shell are the same as those used with the Bourne shell. Additionally, in the C shell, values assigned to certain local variables automatically update the environment variable of the same name. These variables include the following:

path — The search path. Updates *PATH*.

home — Your home directory; updates *HOME*. On login, the shell automatically assigns a value to this variable.

term — Your terminal type. Updates *TERM*.

If you want to change your *PATH*, you should assign a value to *path* instead of *PATH*. To update the value of *path*, use a command like this:

```
$ set path = (/bin /usr/bin $home/bin $home . $path) ⏎
$ _
```

In the above example, the `set` command is used instead of `setenv`. Use `set` to assign values to local (nonenvironmental) shell variables. The parentheses group the values to be assigned to *path*. With some C shell implementations, you need spaces around the equal sign.

When the local *path* variable is changed, the value is automatically exported to *PATH*; updating *PATH* automatically changes *path*. This feature is provided for your convenience.

Unlike the Bourne shell, much of a C shell's configuration is performed with local shell variables. Use the `set` command to assign values to these configuration variables. An example:

```
$ set autologout = 60 ↵
```

The *autologout* shell variable specifies the maximum number of minutes that a shell may be unused before it automatically exits. In the above example the shell automatically executes the `exit` command after one hour.

To view the values for all local variables, use the `set` command with no arguments. This works much like `set` in the Bourne shell.

Two other important shell variables are *prompt* and *history*. The *prompt* variable's value defines the C shell prompt. For example, to change your shell prompt to CMD:

```
$ set prompt = "CMD: " ↵
CMD: _
```

C shell tracks the number of commands (called *events*) you have executed. To display the event number as part of the prompt, include an exclamation point in the prompt string. Here is one way to include the event number in the prompt string:

```
CMD: set prompt = "\!> " ↵
24> _
```

You must precede the exclamation point with a backslash to prevent the C shell from interpreting the character immediately. The C shell uses the exclamation point to indicate a command history reference.

Command History
You can configure the C shell to maintain a history stack to remember the commands you execute. The value in the *history* shell variable specifies the number of commands to remember. For example, to remember the last 20 commands you have executed:

```
24> set history = 20 ⏎
25> _
```

To view the contents of the history stack, use the C shell command history. An example of a history stack follows:

```
29> history ⏎
    25 ls
    26 pwd
    27 vi /etc/inittab
    28 grep tty /etc/inittab | wc -l
    29 history
30> _
```

Notice that each command in the list is preceded by its event number. You can reference any event in the history stack by specifying an historical reference, which is always preceded by an exclamation point.

You can obtain an historical reference in one of three ways:

❏ By specifying the event number. The form of this reference is !*n*, where *n* is the event number. For example, !22 references event number 22.

❏ By specifying the position in the history stack relative to the current event. The form of this reference is !-*m*, where *m* is the number of events before the current event. For example, !-4 references the command executed four events before the current event. A special form of this reference is !!, which is the same as !-1.

❏ By specifying part of the event's command text. The form of this reference is !*q*, where *q* is enough text to match the event you want to execute. For example, !vi matches the most recent vi event and !t matches the most recent event starting with the letter *t*. The search for this event begins at the bottom of the list (the event with the largest number) and proceeds backward until either the first matching reference is located or the top of the list is found. **NOTE:** If you specify too few letters, you may not execute the command you want; if you use this form, specify as many letters as possible to identify the desired command.

You may use any of the reference methods to execute a particular event. Returning to the previous example, the current event number is 30. To reexecute event 28, you can use any of the following three references: !28, !-2, or !g.

Let's reexecute event 26:

```
30> !26 ⏎
pwd
/users/demo
31> _
```

Notice that the shell displays the interpretation of the event reference before executing the event. Regardless of the form of the historical reference,
the C shell interprets and then echoes the event. If the C shell cannot resolve an historical reference, the shell displays an error message:

```
31> !12 ⏎
12: Event not found.
31> _
```

If the shell cannot resolve the historical reference, it does not execute the
event, the bad reference is not placed into the history stack, and the event
number does not change.

You may also reuse arguments from different events in the history stack to
form new commands to execute. For example, suppose the history stack
contains the following:

```
41 nroff -man /usr/man/man1/ls.1 | more
42 more /etc/inittab
43 vi hello.c
```

In case you are curious, nroff(1) is a text formatting utility available with
many UNIX systems. Refer to your system's documentation for more information.

To run more on hello.c, you could execute the following:

```
44> more !$ ⏎
```

The !$ references the last argument from the previous event. When a com-
mand executes, the pieces of the command are numbered from left to right,
starting with 0. The last argument can be referenced using the dollar sign,
as shown above.

For example, in event number 41 of the history stack a few paragraphs
back, argument 2 is /usr/man/man1/ls.1. To display this file without retyping the name of the file, you could enter:

```
47> more !41:2 ⏎
```

Another way to perform this command:

```
47> more !nr:2 ⏎
```

Remember, the `!nr` matches the most recent event beginning with *nr*, which was event 41. You may use more than one event's arguments to create a new command. For example:

```
48> !47:0 !43$ !nroff:2 ⏎
more hello.c /usr/man/man1/ls.1
   .
   .
   .
```

In this example, the command from event 47 (`more`) is executed on the last argument from event 43 (`hello.c`) and the second argument from the most recent event beginning with the letters *nroff* (which was event 41; this particular argument is `/usr/man/man1/ls.1`). The example is ridiculous; however, it shows the usefulness of this feature.

If you want to use several consecutive arguments from a single event, you can specify an argument range as part of the event reference. For example, to `cat` (remember, `cat` copies information to stdout) the files in event 48, you could do this:

```
49> cat !48:1-$ ⏎
cat hello.c /usr/man/man1/ls.1
   .
   .
   .
```

In this example, the range `1-$` indicates all arguments from argument 1 through the last argument. Using just `!48` is the same as using `!48:0-$`. Since event 48 had only two arguments, the command can also be executed like this:

```
49> cat !48:1-2 ⏎
```

You can also change an event in the history stack and execute this changed command. The general syntax for this change is:

```
event:s/old/new/ ⏎
```

In this syntax, *event* is an historical reference (for example !41 or !nr), *old* is the piece of the command to change, and *new* is the replacement text that replaces *old*. The :s implies a substitution; a similar syntax is also used by vi, as you will see in Chapter 8.

An example of how to correct an improperly typed command? Okay:

```
50> mroe hello.c ⏎
mroe: No such file or directory
51> _
```

To change mroe to more without retyping the command, do this:

```
51> !!:s/mroe/more/ ⏎
```

This example references the previous event in the history stack, changes the *first* occurrence of mroe to more, and executes the resulting command. To change a portion of the previous event, you can use circumflexes to specify the substitution. For example:

```
51> ^mroe^more ⏎
```

The C shell interprets the ^ delimiters to indicate that a substitution should be performed on the previously executed event.

Remember event 41?

```
45> history ⏎
    41 nroff -man /usr/man/man1/ls.1 | more

    .
    .
    .
```

For a more complex substitution, change the file in event 41 to /usr/man/man3/string.3c. To perform this substitution, you could do this:

```
52> !41:s/1\/ls.1/3\/string.3c ⏎
```

Pretty ugly, huh? The backslashes differentiate the slashes used in the substitution text, which are preceded by backslashes, from the slashes used as separators in the substitution command, which are not. This form of event substitution requires some practice.

A prettier and easier way to perform this command:

```
52> !41:s^1/ls.1^3/string.3c ←┘
```

You may use any substitution separator (for example, % or @; don't use !), but you must use it consistently within the substitution.

To substitute *new* text for every occurrence of *old* in an historical reference, precede the substitution command with the letter *g* (global). For example, to replace all occurrences of .txt with .doc in event 38:

```
53> !38:gs/.txt/.doc/ ←┘
```

You may also use the substitution modifier on a particular argument of an historical reference:

```
54> more !39:3:s/mr/rm/ ←┘
```

In this example, the third argument in event 39 has the letters *mr* replaced by *rm* and the resulting argument is used when more executes.

Normally, when you log out of the C shell, the contents of your history stack are lost. You can retain the last *n* events in your history stack between C shell sessions by executing the following command:

```
set savehist = n
```

On logout from the shell, the last *n* events present in the history stack are written to the file $HOME/.history. On login, these events are read to initialize the history stack, and the first command you execute is event number *n*+1. You should use vi to add this command to your .cshrc file; if you are unsure how to do this, wait until you read Chapter 6.

Aliases

If you find that you are always using the same options with a specific command, entering these options each time you execute the command is a waste of time. The C shell provides a way to create *aliases* (synonyms) for commands and their options. For example, the command /bin/ls -lF (a long directory listing with filename formatting) can be aliased to llf:

```
53> alias llf /bin/ls -lF ←┘
```

Once the alias is executed, any time that the command llf is entered, the C shell interprets the command to mean /bin/ls -lF. For example:

```
54> llf /usr/spool/lp ←┘
```

```
total 20
-rw-rw-r--   1  lp       lp           0  Apr 27  11:13   SCHEDLOCK
d---rwx---   3  bin      lp          48  Jun 25   1989   admins/
d---rwx---   2  bin      lp         160  Jun 25   1989   bin/
-rw-rw-r--   1  lp       lp           4  Feb 19  22:25   default
d---rwx---   4  bin      lp          80  Apr 27  11:13   fifos/
d---rwx---   2  bin      lp          64  Jan 26  19:48   logs/
d---rwx---   2  bin      lp         336  Aug 5    1989   model/
d---rwx---   2  bin      lp          80  Apr 27  11:36   requests/
d---rwx---   2  bin      lp          64  Aug 3    1989   system/
d---rwx---   2  bin      lp         240  Apr 27  11:36   temp/
-rw-r--r--   1  lp       lp           6  Aug 18   1989   users
55> _
```

Unlike history substitutions, the shell does not echo the results from alias substitutions before executing the request. To view an alphabetical list of the aliases you created, use the command `alias` without arguments; each line of the list contains a single alias definition. The first word of each line is the alias, and the meaning follows.

Some example aliases:

```
55> alias ⏎
a alias
h history
llf /bin/ls -1F
print pr -e6 !* | lp
rm mv !* /tmp
stop kill -9
56> _
```

The first alias in the list shortens the `alias` command.

The second alias provides a shorter command for viewing the contents of the history stack.

The third alias is the one created in the previous example.

The fourth alias defines the `print` command to format, using pr(1), and print any files passed as arguments (`!*` specifies all arguments following the alias executed). For example, using the `print` alias

```
27> print file1 file2 ⏎
```

executes the command:

```
pr -e6 file1 file2 | lp
```

To create this particular alias, the following command was used:

```
23> alias print 'pr -e6 \!* | lp' ↵
```

The single quotes surround the alias value to prevent the C shell from interpreting the asterisk; the backslash precedes the ! to prevent the shell from interpreting the request as a history substitution.

The fifth alias in the list causes the rm command to move files to the /tmp directory. The alias provides a primitive method for preventing you from unintentionally deleting your files.

The final alias creates the stop command to kill all programs whose process identification numbers are specified as arguments to the command. For example, stop 8400 performs the command kill -9 8400.

You can create an alias that has the same sequence of characters as a regular UNIX command. To use the command instead of the alias, either precede the command with a backslash or specify the entire directory path for the command. For example, to use the real rm command instead of the alias rm, use either \rm or /bin/rm.

When the shell interprets a command, each argument of the command is checked to see if it is an alias; if so, the shell replaces the argument immediately with the contents of the alias. If an alias references arguments from the command (for example, by using !*), these argument references are fulfilled before the remainder of the command's arguments are interpreted, which is how the print alias above works.

You should define all aliases in your .cshrc file, since aliases are not automatically inherited by any subsequent shells. If you are unsure about how to add these commands to a .cshrc file, wait until you get to Chapter 6.

To remove an alias, use the unalias command. For example, to remove the stop alias, enter the following:

```
56> unalias stop ↵
57> _
```

To view the assignment for a specific alias, use the alias command with the name of the alias to view as the only argument. For example:

```
59> alias print
pr -e6 !* | lp
60> _
```

Redirection of stderr

As discussed earlier in this chapter, you can redirect stderr for any command. Unlike the Bourne shell, unfortunately, the C shell cannot redirect stderr independently of stdout.

To redirect stderr to the same location as stdout, place an ampersand after the redirection selected.

NOTE: The use of the ampersand to redirect stderr differs from its use to place a command into background mode (see Chapter 3 and later in this chapter). The syntax of the command determines how the shell interprets the ampersand.

For example, to redirect stderr and stdout from *command* to file, use:

```
61> command >& file ⏎
```

And, yes, appending the stderr and stdout from *command* to file is performed like this:

```
61> command >>& file ⏎
```

To pipe stdout and stderr from *command* to stdin for *command2*:

```
61> command |& command2 ⏎
```

Redirecting stdin or (only) stdout is the same as described in Chapter 3.

By the way, if you want to prevent the shell from overwriting a file without informing you, do the following:

```
62> set noclobber ⏎
```

Then, if a file by the same name exists, attempting to overwrite it via stdout redirection results in this:

```
63> cat - > file ⏎
file: File Exists
64> _
```

Once *noclobber* is set, redirection to an existing file requires you to place an exclamation point after the redirection symbol:

```
64> cat - >! file ←
This is an overwrite ←
^D
65> _
```

Remember, you need the CTRL-D (^D) to terminate `cat`. Appending to a file via >> also requires the exclamation point if the file exists; otherwise, the shell reports an error.

To turn off the *noclobber* flag, use the `unset` command:

```
65> unset noclobber ←
```

Job Control

When you request that the C shell execute a command, you are creating a *job*. A job is the execution of one or more commands that are started as a single unit. For example, the command

```
66> pr file | lp ←
```

is one job, although two processes are created to complete the task.

A job always starts in one of two states: foreground or background. For a discussion of foreground and background processes, see Chapter 3. Most jobs you execute run in foreground.

To execute a command in background mode, type an ampersand after the command. For example:

```
70> pr file1 file2 | lp -s & ←
[1] 1231 1232
71> _
```

The number in square brackets is the job number. The numbers after the job number are the process identification numbers (PID numbers). In the example, both process 1231 (the `pr` command) and process 1232 (the `lp` command) are part of job 1.

You can configure the C shell to inform you when a background job is done. To configure the C shell to provide this information, use `vi` to add the following line to your `.cshrc` file:

```
set notify
```

If you are unsure about how to add commands to `.cshrc`, wait until you have read Chapter 6. If the background job completes successfully, this message appears:

```
[1] Done     pr file1 file2 | lp -s
```

If the background job terminates abnormally, the completion message resembles this:

```
[1] Exit 1     pr file1 file2 | lp -s
```

By accident, you might start a long job in foreground mode. Some UNIX implementations provide job control to let you easily change a foreground job into a background job.

Systems that provide job control also provide a third job state: *suspended*. A suspended job is one that is not running but is still present in the system. With job control, you can change a job's state from foreground to suspended to background and back.

To suspend a job running in the foreground, press the defined suspend character. You can define the suspend character using the `stty(1)` field susp. To define the suspend character as CTRL-Z, do this:

```
72> stty susp \^Z
73> _
```

To demonstrate job control, let's start a long job:

```
73> du / > /tmp/t1
```

The `du(1)` command checks each directory listed and reports on the number of disk blocks in use. The command executes recursively on each directory listed, so specifying the root directory, as in the example, checks each directory of the entire file system.

To suspend this job, press CTRL-Z. The shell responds like this:

```
Stopped
74> _
```

A suspended job is still present in the system, but it is not being executed. To view all suspended and background jobs outstanding for your shell, use the jobs command:

```
74> jobs ⏎
[1] +Stopped du / > /tmp/t1
75> _
```

The plus sign indicates that this job was the most recently executed task. A minus sign indicates that the job was the second most recently executed task.

To move the most recently executed suspended job to background state, do the following:

```
75> bg ⏎
[1] +du / > /tmp/t1 &
76> _
```

To move the most recently executed job from background to foreground, do this:

```
76> fg ⏎
du / > /tmp/t1
```

The shell now waits for you to interrupt the job with BREAK or your stty intr character, for you to suspend the job again, or for the job to complete.

If more than one job has been started for a particular shell, you can refer to each job by prefacing the job number with a percent sign. For example, to change job number 3 to foreground:

```
77> %3 ⏎
```

Another way to execute this command:

```
77> fg %3 ⏎
```

To change job number 5 from suspended state to background state:

```
78> bg %5 ⏎
[5] find . -print > t2 &
79> _
```

Here's another way to execute this command:

```
78> %5 &  ⏎
[5] find . -print > t2 &
79> _
```

To interrupt and abort a job before it completes, use the kill(*1*) command with the job number as the argument. For example, to abort job number 2, enter the following:

```
79> kill -9 %2  ⏎
[2] Killed      prog1 file_1
80> _
```

The message displayed by the shell indicates that job number 2 has been killed.

You can also identify a job by the command that the job executed. For example, to kill the du job started earlier in this section, you could enter:

```
80> kill -9 %du  ⏎
[1] Killed      du / > /tmp/t1
81> _
```

NOTE: If you attempt to log out while suspended jobs are pending, the shell warns you that there are stopped jobs. When you log out, all suspended jobs are aborted.

More C Shell Features

The C shell provides many more features than I have discussed so far. This section discusses a few features you may find helpful.

If you want to use your home directory in a filename, use the tilde followed by a slash. For example, to reference the file $HOME/bin/prog1, you can type ~/bin/prog1. If you want to reference the home directory for another user, use the tilde followed by the user's account name. For example, the contents of the home directory for user Jack can be listed with ls ~jack.

To remove a setting for a shell variable, use the unset command. For example, here's how to turn off job control notification:

```
90> unset notify  ⏎
```

When you assign a value to the *path* variable, the C shell searches for all commands and programs within this path and creates an internal table; this table decreases the time required for the shell to start a requested command or program.

If you install a new program in one of the directories in your search path, the shell does not automatically add this program to its internal table. Accordingly, the shell may not find the command when you attempt to execute it.

To recreate the internal table, use this command:

```
86> rehash ⏎
87> _
```

If you change your .cshrc or .login file and want to see the effects of running the changes, you have two options:

1. Log out and then log back in.

2. Use the source command.

The source command executes a C shell file and updates your current shell environment based on the contents of the file. Note that none of the commands executed from this file (or any other C shell script) is placed in your history stack.

Logging Out of a C Shell

You can choose from among four ways provided for logging out of a C shell:

1. Enter the command exit.

2. Enter the command logout (only if the shell is your login shell).

3. Wait for the automatic logout feature, if it is enabled.

4. Press CTRL-D.

Since it is too easy to type CTRL-D by mistake, you can disable this method. To prevent CTRL-D from logging you out of a C shell, use vi to add the following command to your .cshrc file:

```
set ignoreeof
```

When this shell variable is set, CTRL-D causes the shell to display the following message:

```
Use "exit" to logout
```

On logout, the C shell executes the commands in the file $HOME/.logout. This file should contain any commands you want to execute automatically when you exit your account. For example, if you or the applications you use create files in a temporary directory, include the rm command in your .logout file to remove any files remaining in the temporary directory.

You can also use .logout to clear the contents of your screen with either the echo(1) command (to echo the particular escape sequence that clears your terminal's screen) or, if your UNIX system provides, the clear(1) command.

The instructions in your .logout file are the final commands executed by the C shell before you exit your account.

Pop Quiz Time

Yeah, I hate pop quizzes too. How about a quick review of the C shell commands and functions learned in this chapter? See Table 5-1.

Table 5-1. C Shell Commands and Functions

C Shell Commands	
Command	**Function**
alias	Without arguments, this command displays the current list of aliases. With arguments, it defines an alias.
fg, bg	Changes a background or suspended job to foreground mode, or changes a suspended job to background mode.
history	Displays the current history stack.
jobs	Displays a list of all background and suspended jobs you have created.

Table 5-1. C Shell Commands and Functions (continued)

C Shell Commands (continued)	
Command	**Function**
rehash	Re-creates the internal list of all commands and programs found in your search path (*path*).
set	Assigns a value to a local shell variable.
setenv	Assigns a value to an environment variable.
unalias	Removes an alias definition.
~/	References your home directory.
Local Variables that Control the Shell (assigned with set)	
Variable	**Function**
autologout	Sets the number of minutes that a shell waits for input before exiting. When your login shell exits, you are logged out.
history	Sets the number of events stored in the history stack.
ignoreeof	Prevents the use of CTRL-D to exit a shell.
noclobber	Prevents you from overwriting a file using redirection. To overcome this setting, use >! instead of > and >>! instead of >> when redirecting output to a file.
notify	Informs you of the completion of a background job.
prompt	Sets the shell prompt string. Can contain \! to include the event number in the prompt.
savehist	Specifies the number of events retained in the history stack between C shell sessions.

Table 5-1. C Shell Commands and Functions (continued)

History Stack Usage	
Command	**Function**
`!!`	Repeats the previous command.
`!#`	Executes event number # in the history stack.
`!q`	Executes the most recent event in the history stack beginning with q (which can be any characters).
`!-#`	Executes the event that had been executed # commands ago. `!!` is the same as `!-1`.
`:s/old/new/`	Substitutes *new* text for *old* in the referenced event. If using `/` is not convenient, any other character may be used (provided the character is used consistently).
`:#`	Selects only argument number # from the event. In addition, the `:s` modifier may be specified to perform a substitution on just that argument. Also, use `:#-#` to specify a range of arguments.
`$`	Specifies only the last argument (for example, `!$` or `!45$`).
`^old^new^`	A special form of the history substitution that executes the last command but changes *old* to *new* before executing. Use this syntax to make a single change to the previous command.

Got all that? Now practice the following:

❑ Change the settings on your shell and determine their effect.

❑ Play with job control, if you have it.

❑ Create incredibly complex (and possibly useless) aliases.

❏ Create and use the history stack.

And now, in the interests of those who may be curious, a brief blurb about the Korn shell.

THE KORN SHELL

The Korn shell (/bin/ksh) was developed in 1982 at AT&T Bell Labs. It provides a highly compatible superset of the features found in the Bourne shell with many of the enhancements found in C shell. As of release 4, the Korn shell is included with UNIX System V.

Like the Bourne shell, the Korn shell reads and executes the commands in your .profile file when you log in. Borrowing from the C shell, the Korn shell also executes the commands from an environment file for each Korn shell you start. To provide more flexibility, the name for this file is obtained from the *ENV* shell variable that is defined and exported in your .profile file. An example value for *ENV* is $HOME/.kshrc.

The Korn shell uses many of the same environment variables as the Bourne and C shells. It also uses some additional shell variables, including these:

HISTSIZE — The number of commands to retain in your history stack, which is always saved to a history file and retained between sessions.

TMOUT — Similar to the C shell *autologout* local variable, this variable specifies how many seconds to wait before exiting a Korn shell.

VISUAL — Like the C shell, you can edit commands found in your history stack and then execute the results. However, unlike the C shell, you use a text editor, such as vi, to perform these changes. This variable specifies the editor you want to use.

The Korn shell uses more than 30 shell variables to control its operation. You may control approximately 20 more options with the set command and the -o option. For example, to prevent yourself from using CTRL-D to exit the shell, use this command:

```
$ set -o ignoreeof ⏎
```

Look vaguely familiar? To turn off an option, use the set command with the option +o.

Additional features of the Korn shell include aliases, job control, and the ~/

to represent your home directory.

The Korn shell permits you to redirect stderr separately from stdout like the Bourne shell. It also provides an option (*noclobber*) to prevent you from overwriting a file unless you want to.

The primary improvement the Korn shell provides over the C shell is the way you handle the history stack. The Korn shell views the history stack as a file about which you can see only the current line unless you use the `history` command. The current command is always the bottom of the stack. To edit the stack, you press the ESC key.

If you are using the `vi`-style editor to modify your stack (as specified by the *VISUAL* environment variable), type `k` to move up through the command history stack and `j` to move down. Once you have found the command you want to change or execute, type `h` to move left and `l` to move right through the command. Type `x` to delete any characters, `i` to insert new characters, and press RETURN to execute the line. Other editing methods and options are possible with the Korn shell; review your documentation for details.

If you want to use the Korn shell as your login shell, review all Korn shell documentation provided with your system.

NOW YOU KNOW...

The history stack, aliases, and job control are not available in the Bourne shell. I always recommend using the C shell or, if it is available and you really want to, the Korn shell, instead of the Bourne shell for your login shell.

To change your login shell, ask your system administrator.

Chapter 6

Shell Programming I

As mentioned in Chapter 5, the UNIX shell script is similar to the DOS batch file: an executable file that contains a series of commands interpreted and performed by the shell. However, DOS does not provide the broad range of batch file commands that UNIX provides for creating shell scripts.

Creating a shell script is called *shell programming*. You nonprogrammers out there are probably asking, "Why do I need to know about shell programming? Why do I need to know *any* programming?" For two reasons:

1. A shell program is a powerful tool, often providing the shortest distance between a problem and its solution.

2. Who else is going to create and customize your .profile, .cshrc, .login, and .logout files?

The goal for this chapter is to show you how to create your own .cshrc, .login, .logout, and .profile files. In Chapter 9, if you want, you can see how to solve other problems using shell programming.

CREATING A SHELL START-UP SCRIPT

A shell script is a normal file containing a series of shell commands. Typically, you will use vi to create these scripts. For example, use cd to change to your home directory. Let's make a backup of your .profile file before we start. Execute the following:

```
$ mv .profile .profile.old ⏎
$ _
```

If you received an error from mv, ignore it. Now edit the new file .profile. Place the following lines in the file:

```
PATH=/bin:/usr/bin:/usr/ucb
```

```
export PATH
echo "The time is now: \c"
date
count=`who | wc -l`
if [ $count -gt 1 ]
then
    count=`expr $count - 1`
    echo "\n$count other users are on the system.\n"
fi
```

Be sure to type the lines *exactly* as listed. Save the changes you made to the file (use `:w!`) and exit the editor.

You could test this script by logging out and then logging back in; however, this process is time-consuming. Instead, make `.profile` executable:

```
$ chmod +x .profile ⏎
```

Chmod(*1*), which changes the permissions on a file, was described in Chapter 2. Now you can execute `.profile`:

```
$ ./.profile ⏎
The time is now: Tue Apr 17 22:02:28 EDT 1990

2 other users are on the system.
```

If you had an error in the file, you may receive the message

```
syntax error
```

Don't fret. Check the file against the listing shown above, correct any errors you see, and run `.profile` again.

Once your `.profile` returns output similar to the lines shown, congratulate yourself! You've just created a shell script. You may have no idea how it does what it did, but we'll get to that in a moment.

GENERALLY SPEAKING

This chapter discusses only a few shell commands. These commands involve shell variables, covered in Chapter 3, and conditional comparisons. A *conditional comparison* asserts a stipulation, for example that a particular file exists or the current number of users is greater than 1. If the stipulation is true, then one set of commands may be executed; otherwise, another set of commands may be executed.

As you may have noticed, Bourne shell commands differ from C shell commands. This chapter addresses both sets of commands. All Bourne shell commands discussed in this book are documented in the *UNIX Reference Manual* entry for sh(*1*); all C shell commands discussed in this chapter are documented in the entry for csh(*1*).

Before covering shell-specific commands, here are some general programming considerations:

❑ The # anywhere in a line — except within a quoted string — begins a comment. All characters including and after the # are ignored until the end of the line.

❑ Shell scripts are interpreted sequentially; one line must complete before the next line executes.

❑ Use double quotes (") to delimit a string of text containing blanks (for example, "Hello there"). Use single quotes to prevent the shell from interpreting any shell wildcard characters (* and ? are interpreted as wildcards, but '*' and '?' are not).

❑ To extend a command onto the next line in the file, terminate the line with a backslash. Don't split quoted strings across lines.

❑ To reference any shell variable, either local or environmental (exported), precede the variable name with a dollar sign.

❑ C shell scripts are distinguished by a pound sign (#) as the first character in the first line of the script. The first line of a Bourne shell script should be either blank or a command, or a space should precede the pound sign in the first line.

If you don't want to use a real command for the first line of a Bourne shell script, use the colon command, which performs no operation. Be sure to leave a space after the colon. Any characters on the line after the colon and the space are not interpreted. The most common use for this command is the line

```
: /bin/sh
```

This command performs no operation, but it does identify the script to readers as a Bourne shell script.

❑ Beware of slight differences between echo(1), which is executed from /bin/echo, and the echo command provided with each shell. The echo shell command, which is documented in both the sh(1) and the csh(1) entries, has different features depending on the shell selected.

❑ Any shell scripts you create (except for the shell's start-up scripts) must have execute permission (otherwise, you can't run them). Use chmod(1) to add this permission to your script files.

Time to see how to use the commands that comprise the Bourne shell and C shell start-up scripts.

BOURNE SHELL PROGRAMMING

To start, let's examine the .profile you entered earlier:

```
1   PATH=/bin:/usr/bin:/usr/ucb
2   export PATH
3   echo "The time is now: \c"
4   date
5   count=`who | wc -l`
6   if [ $count -gt 1 ]
7   then
8     count=`expr $count - 1`
9     echo "\n$count other users are on the system.\n"
10  fi
```

Line by line, the script performs the following:

Line 1 — This line sets the *PATH* shell variable (your search path) to include only the directories /bin, /usr/bin, and /usr/ucb. At present, this value change is local and does not apply to any commands that this file executes.

Line 2 — All commands executed from this script now inherit the value for *PATH*. When .profile executes (when you log in) and exports a variable, its value becomes environmental in the shell itself, and commands you execute later inherit it.

Line 3 — The echo shell command copies its arguments to stdout. By default, the Bourne shell echo outputs a linefeed (\n) once all arguments are copied to stdout. The \c character suppressed the linefeed; subsequent output occurs on the same line as the message displayed by this command.

REMINDER: The Bourne shell echo command may not be the same as the command /bin/echo. The double quotes are used to delimit the entire string.

Line 4 — The date(1) command displays the time and date. The output from this command is terminated by a linefeed, so subsequent output begins on the next line.

Line 5 — The who(1) command displays a list of the users logged in to the system; the -l option causes wc(1) to count the number of lines produced by who. The grave marks cause the who | wc -l commands to execute first; the results from this command are assigned to the variable *count*. *Count* is not exported; the variable and its value are local.

Line 6 — The if command begins a conditional comparison. This comparison uses the test(1) command. Within Bourne shell scripts, you can invoke the test command by enclosing the arguments for the test in square brackets. More on test in a moment.

Here is the general format for the if construct:

```
if condition1
then
    commands_1
elif condition2
then
    commands_2
    .
    .
    .
else
    commands_n
fi
```

The constructs elif (else if) and else are optional, depending on the requirements of your script. The first condition that evaluates as true determines the particular commands executed. If none of the conditions is true, then the commands after the else statement (if present) are executed.

The conditions you use do not need to be test(1); a condition may be any command you want to execute. UNIX commands return 0 when successful, and successful commands are considered true. For example, you could use grep, which returns 0 only if a line is matched. However, you probably will use test for most of your conditions.

In line 6, if the value stored in *count* is greater than 1, the commands on lines 8 and 9 execute.

Line 7 — The if statement must be followed by a then statement to begin the block of commands executed when the corresponding if condition returns true.

Line 8 — The command expr(1) provides computations within Bourne shell scripts. The result of this line is to subtract one from *count* and assign the results back into *count*. The Bourne shell cannot perform arithmetic; you must use expr(1) for any mathematical computations.

Line 9 — This line echoes a message stating the number of other users on the system. The message is both preceded and followed by an extra linefeed (\n).

Line 10 — All if constructs must be terminated by a fi statement (fi is if backward).

The remainder of this section details the constructs shown in this script (plus a few others).

Shell Parameters

In addition to the shell variables you can create, the shell provides certain built-in variables, called *shell parameters*, that provide status and system information. Access to these parameters is similar to that of shell variables. However, you cannot directly change the values for these parameters.

Chapter 9 discusses several shell parameters. For now, you need to know only two:

$? — The status value returned from the previously executed command. All UNIX commands return a status value; successfully executed commands usually return 0 for this value.

$$ — The process identification number (PID) of the shell.

Here are some examples you can try to show off these variables:

```
$ echo $$ ⏎
417
$ _
```

In this example, the value for the shell parameter *$$* was the PID number for the shell, not for the process created to perform the echo. Inside a shell script, *$$* contains the PID number for the process running the script. For shell start-up scripts, *$$* contains the PID number for the shell itself. This may seem a little confusing; just remember that the process that interprets the *$$* is the one whose PID number is returned.

Let's keep going:

```
$ echo $? ↵
0
$ cat jkfdjdfjkldfsd ↵
cat: jkfdjdfjkldfsd: No such file or directory
$ echo $? ↵
2
$ _
```

The first echo of the shell parameter *$?* displays the status value from echo *$$*. This command executed successfully, so the last return value is 0. The cat command is then attempted on a nonexistent file and fails. The status value is then shown again and is 2, indicating failure.

Conditional Comparisons

The example .profile shown earlier in this chapter includes the following segment of code:

```
if [ $count -gt 1 ]
then
    count=`expr $count - 1`
    echo "\n$count other users are on the system.\n"
fi
```

In the first line the brackets indicate test(1). This example could also have been written like this:

```
if test $count -gt 1
then
    count=`expr $count - 1`
    echo "\n$count other users are on the system.\n"
fi
```

The general format for the if statement is as follows:

```
if condition1
then
    commands_1
```

```
elif condition2
then
    commands_2

        .

        .

        .

else
    commands_n
fi
```

If the result of *conditon1* (in the example, *condition1* is `test $count -gt 1`) is true, *commands_1* is executed. Otherwise, *condition2* is executed. If the result of this command is true, *commands_2* is executed. If *condition2* is not true, condition checking continues either until one returns true or until the `else` statement is encountered. The `else` statement begins the set of commands to execute when all conditions do not return true.

As mentioned earlier, the command most used as a condition is `test`, a Bourne shell command that has this syntax:

```
test expression
```

The `test` expressions you will use most often are shown in Table 6-1.

Table 6-1. Common Test Expressions

Expression	Returns true when...
-r *file* -w *file* -x *file*	The specified file is readable, writable, or executable. Use this test to determine whether you can read from the file, write to the file, or execute the file.
-f *file*	The specified file is a regular file, not a directory, named pipe, or device file.
-d *file*	The specified file is a directory.
-s *file*	The specified file exists and has a size greater than 0.

Table 6-1. Common Test Expressions (continued)

Expression	Returns true when ...
-z *string*	The specified string has a length of zero; that is, it contains no characters. One use for this expression is to determine if a command returns any information. For example, the expression `-z "` `grep -l permit *.doc` `"` returns true if none of the files with suffix *.doc* contain the string *permit*.
-n *string*	The specified string contains at least one character. The opposite of the -z test.
s1 = s2	The specified string s1 is equal to string s2. To test for inequality, use s1 != s2.

n1 -op n2	The specified integers n1 and n2 favorably compare for -op, where -op is one of these:
	
	    -eq (equal)
	    -ne (not equal)
	    -gt (greater than)
	    -lt (less than)
	    -le (less than or equal to)
	    -ge (greater than or equal to)

You can combine these expressions with the operators listed in Table 6-2 to create more complex tests.

Table 6-2. Operators for More Complex Tests

Operator	Effect
!	Negate the following expression. For example, if *$str* is a string, then `! -z "$str"`

Table 6-2. Operators for More Complex Tests (continued)

Operator	Effect
	is the same test as `-n "$str"`
`-a` `-o`	Binary operators AND (`-a`) or OR (`-o`) for combining expressions. When evaluating the combination, `-a` has a higher precedence than `-o`. For example, to test whether the status value returned from the last command was either -1 or -2, use: `$? -eq -1 -o $? -eq -2`

How do you use these operations in a shell script? Try this:

```
if [ -x /usr/local/bin/testprog ]
then
    echo "Running testprog"
    /usr/local/bin/testprog
    if [ $? -ne 0 ]
    then
        echo "testprog failed with exit code $?."
    else
        echo "testprog successfully completed."
    fi
else
    echo "testprog is not available."
fi
```

In this example, a program `/usr/local/bin/testprog` is checked to see if it exists and if you are permitted to execute it (using the `-x` test). If the file exists and is executable, the program is run. Once the program completes, the status value it returned (in *$?*) is checked. Based on this status value, a message is generated.

If /usr/local/bin/testprog does not exist or you cannot execute it, the example generates this message:

```
testprog is not available.
```

Practice making test expressions. Remember that all operators must be delimited by spaces, since all operators are separate arguments for test. One way to create practice test expressions is to enter commands like these at your shell prompt:

```
$ test -x /usr/bin/vi ⏎
$ echo $? ⏎
0
$ _
```

In the example, the test command checks for the existence of /usr/bin/vi (the vi program). The second line displays the result from the test; the result is 0, which indicates that the test was successful and the file is present.

Time to Create Your Own .profile

If you have been doing the examples in this chapter, you may now have a file .profile.old in your home directory. If so, rename (mv) this file to .profile and review its contents for some ideas about the commands to execute when you start a Bourne shell.

If you do not have a .profile.old file, don't worry. You can use the following listing as a guide for creating a .profile file:

```
PATH=/bin:/usr/bin:/usr/ucb:$HOME/bin:.:/usr/local/bin
TZ=EST5EDT
EDITOR=/usr/bin/vi
TERM=vt100
PS1= "Shell> "
SHELL=/bin/sh
export PATH TZ EDITOR TERM PS1 SHELL
umask 022
#
# Set up your terminal communications line
#
stty sane erase \^H intr \^C -ignbrk brkint echoe tab3
```

The first seven lines of the listing establish and export values for some important Bourne shell variables. A umask(1) value is then assigned. The last line uses stty(1) to establish good characteristics for your terminal line* (see Chapter 3 for a discussion of stty).

This sample .profile is okay, but what if you want to use this script to run a set of commands only the first time you log in each day? Add the following lines (without the line numbers, which are present only to help explain the code) to the end of your .profile file:

```
1   cur_date=`date '+%m%d%y'`
2   last_date=""
3
4   if [ -s $HOME/.date ]
5   then
6       last_date=`cat $HOME/.date`
7   fi
8
9   echo "$cur_date" > $HOME/.date
10
11  if [ "$last_date" != "$cur_date" ]
12  then
13      #
14      # Put your commands to execute once today here.
15      #
16  fi
```

An explanation of the important lines in this code follows:

Line 1 — Obtains the current date in a manner that can be easily compared. This execution of the date(1) command returns the current date in the form *MMDDYY*. The result of this command is assigned to the variable *cur_date*.

Line 2 — Initializes *last_date* to an empty string.

Line 4 — Tests to see if you already have a nonempty file named .date in your home directory. If so, then in line 6 the contents of this file are placed in *last_date*.

Line 9 — Places the date that you obtained in line 1 into .date.

Line 11 — Tests to see if *last_date* is different from *cur_date* — in other words, whether the date has changed. If so, then the commands you want to run once each day are executed.

---

*Use the three-character sequence to create the control characters shown in the stty command. For more information, refer to the section in Chapter 3 entitled "Setting Up Your Terminal."

The two strings are quoted just in case one of the strings is empty or contains only blanks. If both strings contain date values, the quotes are not necessary. However, the test [!= 121090] is not syntactically proper. Add the quotes to make the test ["" != "121090"], which can be correctly evaluated.

Lines 13 through 15 — Place as many commands as you want to execute into the script at this location.

The first time this script runs today, .date will contain the previous day's date. Line 9 replaces this date with today's date, so the next time the script executes today, the comparison in line 11 results in *false* and the commands are not executed.

Well, that's how to create a .profile file.

C SHELL PROGRAMMING

Now it's time to show you how to create the C shell start-up and logout scripts. Back at the beginning of this chapter, I discussed this Bourne shell script:

```
1   PATH=/bin:/usr/bin:/usr/ucb
2   export PATH
3   echo "The time is now: \c"
4   date
5   count=`who | wc -l`
6   if [ $count -gt 1 ]
7   then
8       count=`expr $count - 1`
9       echo "\n$count other users are on the system.\n"
10  fi
```

Just to show you the differences between a C shell script and a Bourne shell script, here is the C shell version:

```
1   # Required comment line, because C shell scripts
2   # need a # in column 1 of the first line
3   set path = (/bin /usr/bin /usr/ucb)
4   echo -n "The time is now: "
5   date
6   set count = `who | wc -l`
7   if ( $count > 1 ) then
8       @ count- -
```

```
9     echo "\n$count other users are on the system.\n"
10 endif
```

Seems both similar and different at the same time? Here's a line-by-line discussion of the C shell script:

Lines 1 and 2 — Comment lines are similar between the two shells. However, to differentiate C shell scripts from Bourne shell scripts, C shell scripts must start with a pound sign in column 1 of the first line of the file. Your start-up scripts (.cshrc, .login, and .profile) and your logout script (.logout) are exempt from this rule.

Line 3 — This line assigns a value to the *path* variable. This value is automatically copied to *PATH* and then exported.

Line 4 — The echo shell command differs slightly between the Bourne shell and the C shell. In the C shell, to suppress the terminating linefeed, include the -n option.

Line 5 — Nothing different about executing the date(1) command.

Line 6 — Setting the value for a C shell local variable is slightly different from setting a Bourne shell variable. You *must* include the set keyword as part of the command.

Line 7 — The if construct differs between the Bourne shell and the C shell. The C shell understands complex expressions that are similar to those used by the C programming language; more on these expressions in a moment.

Another difference between the if constructs is that the C shell requires the then keyword on the same line as the if keyword.

Two forms of the if construct are available within the C shell. The first form is this:

```
if ( condition1 ) then
    command_list1
else if ( condition2 ) then
    command_list2
        .

        .

        .

    else
        command_list
    endif
```

The constructs `else if` and `else` are optional, depending on the requirements of your script. The particular *command_list* executed is determined by the first condition comparison that evaluates as true; if none of the conditions evaluate as true, then the *command_list* after the `else` statement, if present, is executed.

The second form of the `if` construct is this:

```
if ( condition ) command
```

This form is useful only if you have exactly one command to execute as a result of the condition evaluating as true.

In line 7 of the example, if the value stored in *count* is greater than 1, the commands in lines 8 and 9 are executed.

Line 8 — Instead of using `expr(1)`, the C shell is capable of performing numeric calculations on integers (numbers without decimal points). Numerical calculations are always preceded by an at sign (@). This particular line decreases by one the value stored in the variable *count*.

Line 9 — Echoes the message stating the number of users. No difference here.

Line 10 — All multiline `if` constructs must be terminated by an `endif` statement.

Similar yet different. Let's create and execute this script. First, in case you already have a `.cshrc` file, let's make a backup of it. Use `cd` to change to your home directory, if necessary.

```
$ mv .cshrc .cshrc.old ⏎
$ _
```

Now, use `vi` to create and edit `.cshrc`. Place the lines from the previous example into the file. Do not include the line numbers. When you have typed the example into the file, save the file and exit `vi`.

To execute this `.cshrc` file, execute a C shell. You will receive output similar to the following:

```
$ /bin/csh ⏎
The time is now: Sun Apr 15 12:42:23 EDT 1990
```

```
2 other users are on the system.


$ _
```

As in the Bourne shell, if you did not type the file correctly, you will receive an error message from the shell. Use vi to correct the file, exit the C shell that you just started and try again. Once the script successfully executes, stay in the C shell to execute the examples in the remainder of this chapter.

As in the Bourne shell section, the following sections cover the C shell-specific programming commands that you will probably use when you create your start-up and logout scripts.

C Shell Parameters and Numerical Variables

Like the Bourne shell, the C shell provides not only shell variables but shell parameters. These parameters, unlike the Bourne shell's cryptic notation, have specific names. In the C shell, these parameters are called *built-in variables.*

You can access the current directory from the built-in variable *$cwd*; in the Bourne shell, the only way to access this information is via the pwd(*1*) command. Another built-in C shell variable, *$status*, provides the exit value from the previously executed command, shell, or shell function. As with the Bourne shell, *$$* contains the current process identification number.

Unlike the Bourne shell, the C shell understands numerical variables. A numerical variable is similar to any variable, except that it can also be used in numerical expressions. To assign a value to a numerical variable, use the following syntax:

```
@ name = expression
```

The @ is the numerical assignment equivalent of the set command. It must be separated from the numerical variable's name by a space. Numerical variables can contain only integers (numbers without decimal points).

Expression is either a number or an arithmetic expression, similar to expressions that can be created in most programming languages. These are some of the operators that may be included in the expression:

( )   parentheses to change the order of evaluation
+   addition
-     subtraction
*   multiplication

/   division

%   modulo

You can also increment a numerical variable using @ *name*++ and decrement a numerical variable using @ *name*--. These operations must appear alone on a line.

Some examples of arithmetic expressions follow:

```
@ x = 12
@ x++
@ y = 22
@ yt = $y + 30
@ quant = ($status - 10) * 100
```

Other operators are available for creating expressions; refer to the csh(*1*) manpage for cryptic details.

C Shell Conditional Comparisons

Like the Bourne shell, the C shell includes the if command to provide conditional comparisons. However, the C shell if has a slightly different construct:

```
if ( condition ) then
    command_list
else if ( condition ) then
    command_list
        .

        .

        .

else
    command_list
endif
```

Instead of providing elif, the C shell uses else if. Also, the condition must be enclosed in parentheses. The condition is usually a C shell expression containing one or more of the operations in Table 6-3, listed in order of increasing precedence; a numerical expression is any combination of numerical variables and integers.

Table 6-3. C Shell Conditions

Operation	Function
|| &&	Logical OR (||) and AND (&&). These are used to combine two conditions.
== !=	Comparisons, as strings, between two expressions. These expressions may be either strings or numeric. These two operations test equality and inequality, respectively.
<=, => <, >	Logical comparisons between two numeric expressions. These operations compare less than or equal to, greater than or equal to, less than, and greater than, respectively.
+ -	Addition and subtraction of two numeric expressions.
* / %	Multiplication, division, and the remainder of two numeric expressions. The result is always an integer.
!	Logical "not" of the subsequent expression; an example of the syntax is ! ($count < 12). Basically, if the subsequent expression results in a non-0 value, the result of this operation is 0; if the subsequent expression is 0, the result of this operation is 1.
( )	Encloses an expression in parentheses to force a certain order of execution not provided by the normal order of precedence.

An expression also can be created from a file enquiry of the form *-l filename*, where *filename* is the name of the file to enquire and *l* is one of these:

r — User has read access
w — User has write access
x — User has execution access, or search access if *filename* is a directory
e — The file exists
o — The user owns the file
z — The file exists and has zero size (nothing in it)

f — The file is a regular file
d — The file is a directory

If the file cannot be accessed or does not exist, all enquiries return false.

The condition can also be the result of a set of commands enclosed in braces ({ }). For example, to use grep to verify that a file contains a particular string, you could use the if statement:

```
if ( {grep string filename} ) then
    . . .
```

NOTE: The test(1) command is available only within the Bourne shell and cannot be used to perform conditional comparisons in the C shell.

In C shell expressions, true is any nonzero value; false is 0. This contradicts the return status from a command, which is 0 when the command is successful. Just remember, to the C shell a successful command execution is true regardless of what *$status* reports.

The C shell also provides another way to construct an if statement:

```
if ( condition ) command
```

This form of the if statement is useful if you have a single command to execute for a single condition.

Creating .cshrc, .login, and .logout Files

If you have been doing the examples presented in this chapter, you may now have a file .cshrc.old in your home directory. If so, rename (mv) this file back to .cshrc and review its contents for some ideas about the commands to execute when you start a C shell.

The files .cshrc and .login are executed under the following conditions (see Chapter 5):

.cshrc — For each C shell started

.login — After .cshrc, but only for the login C shell

All variables assigned using setenv and all terminal set-up commands should be placed into .login. All set commands to control the shell (for example, set ignoreeof) and all aliases should be placed into the .cshrc file. Any commands you want to execute automatically before you log out should be placed into .logout.

An example `.login` follows:

```
setenv PATH /bin:/usr/bin:/usr/ucb/bin:$HOME/bin:.:/usr/local/bin
setenv TZ EST5EDT
setenv EDITOR /usr/bin/vi
setenv TERM vt100
setenv SHELL /bin/csh
umask 022
#
# Set up your terminal communications line
#
stty sane erase \^H intr \^C -ignbrk brkint echoe tab3 susp \^Z
```

This example file is similar to the one for `.profile`. The only differences are that `setenv` is used to assign and export the variables and that the shell prompt is not assigned in this file, since it is a shell control variable.

Instead of logging out and logging back in to verify your `.login` script, use the `source` command. This command executes a C shell script as though the script had been executed as part of C shell startup. For example:

```
$ source .login ⏎
$ _
```

An example `.cshrc` file follows:

```
# Define any aliases needed
alias h history
alias pr 'pr -e6 -l80 -f'
alias ls 'ls -FC'
# Set up shell control stuff
set prompt = '\!> '
set history = 25
set ignoreeof
set noclobber
set autologout = 60
```

See Chapter 5 for a discussion of the commands in this example.

I have never found a need for `.logout`. Some people use it to remove any temporary files that their work has created, such as backup files created by a word processor. Creating this file is similar to creating `.login` and `.cshrc`; just use `vi` to place the commands you want to execute into this file.

You now know how to create your C shell start-up and logout files. Just for completeness, you should know how to execute a set of commands once each day using the C shell.

Place these commands without the line numbers into your `.login` file:

```
1    set cur_date = `date '+%m%d%y'`
2    set last_date = ""
3
4    if ( ! -z $home/.date && -e $home/.date ) then
5        set last_date = `cat $home/.date`
6    endif
7
8    echo $cur_date >! $home/.date
9
10   if ( "$last_date" != "$cur_date" ) then
11       #
12       # Put your commands to execute once today here.
13       #
14   endif
```

Some notes on particular lines:

Lines 4 through 6 could have been combined into one long line, as follows:

```
if ( ! -z $home/.date && -e $home/.date ) \
    set last_date = `cat $home/.date`
```

The backslash indicates that both lines are part of a single command. Also notice that `$home` is used instead of `$HOME` to indicate your home directory.

Line 8 uses the `>!` form of redirection in case *noclobber* has been set.

"YOUR MISSION, JIM ..."

Time for you to use your new programming prowess to customize your shell start-up scripts to improve your shell's usability. Once you have configured the shell to your liking, proceed to Chapter 7 to find out about some more useful UNIX utilities.

Chapter 9 provides more information about Bourne shell and C shell programming.

Chapter 7

Some User Utilities

One of the really nice features of UNIX is its abundance of standard utilities. Some of these utilities permit you to execute programs at particular times, some provide interuser communications, and some make using UNIX so much easier to use than other operating systems. I discussed some of the useful utilities, like `lp`, in previous chapters. This chapter describes the time-based and user communications facilities.

YEAH, WRITE

The `write`(1) command permits you to send single-line messages to other users who are logged in at one or more terminals. The message is immediately delivered and displayed on the recipient's terminal.

To use `write` to send a quick message to another user, enter:

```
$ write user ⏎
```

In the above command, *user* is the account name for the recipient of a message. If you are not sure who is logged in, use the `who`(1) command to display the list of current system users.

For example, if you are logged in as account *demo1* and want to send a message to user Jack, enter:

```
$ write jack ⏎
```

The terminal at which Jack is logged in displays a message containing your username, your terminal's device name, and the time. For example:

```
Message from demo1 (tty01) [Fri Apr 27 12:01:29]...
```

Once this message is displayed on Jack's terminal, `write` beeps your terminal twice to indicate that the connection has been made. You may then enter your messages.

The receiving user must invoke `write` to send replies, so expect that a message similar to the one above will be displayed on your terminal.

Once `write` sends the beeps to your terminal, begin typing your message, ending each line by pressing ENTER. When you press ENTER, `write` immediately sends the message to the receiving user (in the example, Jack).

If Jack is sending messages to you at the same time, your terminal displays the messages immediately on receipt. If a message is received while you are creating a message for Jack, your message may appear messed up. However, your message is fine; your terminal looks that way because one message is overwriting the other. Continue to type your message and press ENTER to send it.

Some users invent a protocol to prevent messages from overwriting each other. For example, when you are done with a message, send the characters +*O*+ to indicate to the other user that you are waiting for a response.

While you are in `write`, you can execute a command by starting a line with an exclamation point and then typing the command; `write` invokes a shell to execute the command and returns on completion.

When you are done with a `write` session, press CTRL-D to exit `write` and return to your shell. The recipient terminal receives the message "EOT" to indicate that you have ended the session.

If you want to prevent users from sending you messages, execute this command:

```
$ mesg n ⏎
```

The `mesg`(1) command controls whether messages can be received by your terminal. If you attempt to write to a user who is denying messages, you will receive this message:

```
Permission denied
```

If you are in a `write` session with a user and that user executes `mesg n`, `write` exits the next time you send a message.

In some instances, a user may be logged on at more than one terminal; using `write` to communicate with that user produces the following message:

```
user is logged on more than one place.
You are connected to "terminal1".
```

```
Other locations are:
terminal2
```

If you want to communicate with a user on a particular terminal, execute `write` in the following manner

```
$ write user termname ⏎
```

where *termname* is the name of a terminal on which the user is logged in. Use the `who`(*1*) command to display the names of the terminals at which each user is logged in.

ELECTRONIC MAIL

Electronic mail (e-mail) provides a way to transmit messages, notes, memos, and documents to other users on your own system or on a remote system. These messages are transmitted and received whether or not the receiving user is logged in.

The `mailx`(*1*) command provides a flexible environment for sending and receiving electronic mail. When you send a message, `mailx` lets you review and edit the message prior to transmission; when you receive a message, `mailx` lets you save, delete, and respond to the message.

Some systems provide only the `mail`(*1*) command, which is a much simpler version of `mailx`. Other systems provide only `mailx`, but its program name is `mail`. This discussion covers `mailx` only, since the `mail` manpage entry adequately explains this simpler mail program.

To find out whether you have received any electronic mail messages, type the command:

```
$ mailx ⏎
```

If you have no messages waiting, `mailx` responds with this:

```
No mail in /usr/spool/mail/demo
```

The file shown in the message (`/usr/spool/mail/demo` in the above message; a different message may be displayed for you) is your mailbox, where the electronic mail facility stores incoming messages for your account. The configuration of your e-mail facility determines your mailbox location; your system administrator should have this information. If your administrator doesn't know, refer to the manpage for `mail`(*1*).

To send e-mail to a user on your system, you only need the user's account name. For example, to send e-mail to user Mary, use this command:

```
$ mailx mary ←
```

The program then waits for input from you. Type a message such as this:

```
The meeting today is scheduled for 4:30 p.m. Many ←
apologies, but no other time was available for the ←
room. ←
```

To finish the message and send it, press CTRL-D; `mailx` responds with "EOT" and transmits the message to the specified user.

UNIX systems primarily use one of these two methods for transmitting and receiving e-mail messages:

❏ UUCP, the UNIX-to-UNIX Copy Package. This software, which most UNIX systems include, provides communications between systems connected with modems or serial lines.

❏ If the system is connected to other systems via a local-area or wide-area network, the network services software probably provides a way to send electronic messages to other users on the network.

To send e-mail to a user on another system, ask your UUCP or network administrator for details concerning how to specify the user's account name.

More on sending e-mail in a moment.

Reading Your Electronic Mail

On most systems, the shell login scripts (for example, `/etc/profile`) are configured to inform you of the presence of new e-mail messages, usually with the message:

```
You have mail.
```

If you receive this message, run `mailx`, which displays a list of the messages sent to your account. For example:

```
$ mailx ←
System V Mail (version 3.2)  Type ? for help.
"/usr/spool/mail/demo": 2 messages 2 unread
```

```
 U  2 demo@pwatl.UUCP  Thu Mar 1 17:59   10/243   Another msg to you
>U  1 jtk@pwatl.UUCP    Thu Mar 1 17:54   9/240    This is a message.
```

The displayed information is the *header summary* of the messages in your mailbox. The U in the first column of the header summary indicates that the message has not yet been read. The second column contains the message sequence number. The third column is the name of the user who sent the message. The date and time that the message was received appear in the next column. The fifth column (9/240 for message 1 above) is the number of lines and characters in the message. The last column is the subject line from the message. The right angle bracket (>) beside message 1 identifies it as the current message.

The ? prompt indicates that mailx is in command mode. In command mode, you may delete, read, save, or respond to a message in your mailbox. Commands have the following syntax:

```
command msgs args
```

In this syntax, *command* is the mailx command to execute, *msgs* is a list of messages to manipulate, and *args* are optional arguments based on the requirements of the command. If not specified, the command is print, or type, which displays the selected messages on the screen. If not specified, *msgs* is the current message.

Table 7-1 describes some command mode commands. The bold letters of the command are the minimum abbreviation permitted. Optional arguments are enclosed in square brackets.

Table 7-1. Electronic Mail Command Mode Commands

Command	Action Taken
delete [*msgs*]	Delete the specified messages. Deleted messages may be recovered (until the mailx session ends) with the undelete command.
edit [*msgs*]	Place the specified messages in a temporary file and permit the user to edit them.
Forward [*msgs*] *users*	Forward the specified messages to the selected users.

Table 7-1. Electronic Mail Command Mode Commands (continued)

Command	Action Taken
headers [+ |-| msgs]	The header summary is displayed page by page. Without arguments, this command displays the current page of headers. To display the next page of headers, use h +. To display the previous page of headers, use h -. If a set of message numbers (msgs) is specified, only these headers are displayed.
help	When in doubt...
lpr [msgs]	Print the specified messages on the printer via lp. The messages are treated as if you read them using the print or type command.
mail user	Mail a message to a user. This action is the same as invoking mailx from your shell.
pipe [msgs] command | [msgs] command	Pipe a set of messages into a specified shell command.
print [msgs] type [msgs]	Display the messages on the screen.
quit	Exit mail.
reply [msg]	Send a reply to the author of a specific message.
save [msgs] filename	Save the msgs in the file specified by filename.
set name set name=value	Define a mailx control variable. These control variables are described later in this chapter.
!command	Execute the specified shell command.
shell	Start an interactive shell, such as /bin/csh. This command determines which shell to start from the SHELL environment variable.

Table 7-1. Electronic Mail Command Mode Commands (continued)

Command	Action Taken
undelete [*msgs*]	Recover the specified messages that you deleted with the delete command during this mailx session.
unset name	Remove the definition for a mailx control variable. Mailx control variables are discussed later in this chapter.

The table lists only the most useful mailx commands. Refer to the mailx(1) documentation for the complete list of available commands.

For these commands, *msgs* is a list of message identifiers separated by spaces. The message identifiers are listed in Table 7-2.

Table 7-2. Message Identifiers

Identifier	Description
n	Message sequence number *n* as shown in the header summary
.	The current message, which the right angle bracket (>) marks in the header summary
$	The last message in the mailbox
*	All messages (most often used with delete or lpr)
n-m	An inclusive list of message sequence numbers between n and m
user	All messages sent by the specified user
:u	All unread messages, marked by U in the header summary

Table 7-2. Message Identifiers (continued)

Identifier	Description
:r	All read messages
:d	All deleted messages

Sample `mailx` commands are listed below:

d *   — Delete all messages.

d :r   — Delete all messages that have been read.

1pr   — Print the current message.

F 2 jtk — Forward message 2 to user jtk.

s 1 jddl — Save message 1 to file jddl.

Once you read a message, it is marked as read. When the `mailx` session ends, all marked messages that were not deleted are moved to a secondary `mailx` message file, called the *mbox* file, which is normally the file `$HOME/mbox`. The mbox file is similar to an archive that you can use to keep track of old e-mail messages.

To read messages from your mbox, use the command:

    $ mailx -f $HOME/mbox ↵

The same commands are available whether `mailx` reads your mbox file or your mailbox file.

Sending Electronic Messages
An example was presented earlier to show you how to send messages to other users. This section gives you more details about sending messages.

An e-mail message may be sent to another user by entering

    $ mailx *user* ↵

and then entering the message to send, terminating with CTRL-D. You may send the same e-mail message to more than one user by including the account name for these users as subsequent command-line arguments. For example, to send an e-mail message to user1, user2, and user3, use the command:

```
$ mailx user1 user2 user3 ⏎
```

Then enter the message and terminate with CTRL-D.

You may use other methods to create e-mail messages, instead of entering the message text followed by CTRL-D. Electronic mail message text is always obtained from stdin; using this feature, you can pipe the results of a shell command into the `mailx` command for transmission to another user. The following example sends the current date to user John:

```
$ echo "The current date is `date`" | mailx john ⏎
```

You may also send the contents of a file as e-mail. For example:

```
$ mailx jill </etc/profile ⏎
```

If you substitute your account name for the example account names and then read the e-mail you send yourself, you will notice that no subject phrase appears in the header summary displayed when you view your e-mail. To include a subject line, use the `-s` option for `mailx`. For example:

```
$ echo "Current Date: `date`" | mailx -s "The Current Date" user ⏎
```

The subject of this message is "The Current Date." The subject string must be enclosed in quotes if it contains any spaces or tabs. You may also specify the `-s` option when using the left angle bracket (<) to obtain the message from the contents of a file.

When `mailx` obtains nonredirected input from stdin, the program places you in *input mode*, where you can enter the message to send.

When you form an e-mail message, it is stored in a message buffer until you are ready to send it. While you are entering text into the buffer, several *tilde commands* are available to permit you to edit and review the message.

A tilde command, so named because the command always begins with the tilde (~), must begin in column 1 of the message. If you enter anything on the line and then back up to column 1 before entering the tilde command, the command is not interpreted; the tilde must be the first character entered on a new line. Note that `mailx` immediately interprets and performs tilde commands. See Table 7-3 for a list of tilde commands.

Table 7-3. Tilde Commands in Mailx

Command	Function
~c *users*	Add the list of users to the carbon copy (cc) list; these users also receive the mail message. All message recipients get the carbon copy list of users. The ~b command specifies blind copy (bcc) lists; recipients of blind copies receive the message without other recipients' knowledge.
~r *file*	Read the contents of the named file into the message buffer.
~h	Permits you to edit the subject line, carbon copy list, blind copy list, and TO list. If a field is displayed with an initial value, you may edit the field as though you had just entered it.
~p	Review the message.
~q	Quit entering this message. If the message buffer contains at least one character, the message is saved to your dead letter file, $HOME/dead.letter.
~s *string*	Set the subject line to the specified string.
~v	Place the contents of the message buffer into a temporary file and permit the user to edit this file. On completion, the contents of the file are placed into the message buffer and you are returned to input mode. This command lets you correct errors in your mail message; otherwise, you cannot correct errors in any line but the current one.
~x	Same as ~q except that the message buffer is not saved in the dead letter file.
~! *command*	Execute the specified shell command and return.

Table 7-3. Tilde Commands in Mailx (continued)

Command	Function
~<!command	Execute the named shell command, inserting the stdout results from the command into the message buffer.
~.	Same as CTRL-D — end of the message.
~?	List all tilde commands available.

Some notes about each command:

❏ The ~r command displays the number of lines and characters inserted into the message buffer from the specified file.

❏ The ~v command places the user in the visual editor of choice. (See the next section, on configuring mailx. By default, vi is used.) Once you are done editing the message, you must save the changes you made and then exit the editor to continue with mailx. On return to mailx, the program displays the word (*continue*) and places you in input mode at the end of the message buffer. Any new text you enter is added to the message immediately following the contents of the edited message buffer.

❏ The ~s command overrides the subject line specified in the -s option.

❏ While you are in input mode, the interrupt character (usually CTRL-C) and BREAK have the same action as ~q. Your terminal's stty(1) settings (the intr character) define your interrupt character. If you want to ignore interrupts (either CTRL-C or BREAK), invoke mailx with the -i option. Use this option to overcome the problems of using mailx from a terminal connected to the computer via a noisy modem line.

❏ The carbon copy list (~c command) specifies users who are also to receive the message. All recipients of this message are informed of the users on the carbon copy list. You can use ~b to specify a blind copy list of users who are to receive the message. Other recipients of the message are not informed that the users on the blind copy list have received the message.

Once the message buffer contains the message you want to send and all recipients have been specified, enter CTRL-D or ~. to send the message.

At some point you may want to send an electronic message containing an object file or program; unfortunately, the e-mail facility is designed to handle only printable ASCII characters. To overcome this problem, some implementations of UNIX include the programs uuencode and uudecode. Uuencode converts a binary file into an ASCII file format suitable for e-mail; uudecode converts this file back to binary.

Configuring Your Electronic Mail Environment

When mailx starts, it reads the file $HOME/.mailrc and executes the commands in the file. These commands are the same as the commands you may execute while reading your incoming messages (that is, command mode commands). You are responsible for creating and maintaining this file.

The commands you place in your .mailrc file are usually those that affect your environment. The most important of these environmental commands is set, which has two forms

```
set name
set name=value
```

where *name* is a control variable. The control variable being set determines the specific form the set command uses. To erase a variable, use the unset command.

Variables not requiring a value are control switches; set the variable to initiate its action. To disable a control switch, either use set and precede the variable name with *no* (for example, set nohold disables the hold switch) or unset the variable.

You may set more than 40 control variables to tailor your mailx environment. Some of these variables are listed in Table 7-4.

Table 7-4. Control Variables in Mailx

Variable	Function
askcc	Prompts for the carbon copy list after a message is entered. The default is *noaskcc.*
asksub	Prompts for the subject before a message is entered. The default is *noasksub.*

Table 7-4. Control Variables in Mailx (continued)

Variable	Function
chron	Causes `mailx` to display messages in chronological order. The most recently received message is shown last. The default is *nochron* (most recently received message shown first).
cmd = `command`	Specifies the default command for the `pipe` (or `|`) command. By default, this variable is not set. If you want the `pipe` command to print the specified messages, set this variable to `/usr/bin/lp`.
crt = `number`	Automatically pipes messages containing more than the specified number of lines into the command specified by the *PAGER* control variable, described below. (Usually, *PAGER* contains the `more` command.) By default, *crt* is not set. For most terminals, a value of 22 is optimal.
DEAD = `name`	Names the file that stores message buffers from interrupted messages. You can interrupt messages by either pressing BREAK, by entering the ~q command while creating a message, or by pressing the interrupt character (specified by the terminal's `stty(1)` settings; usually CTRL-C). By default, this variable is set to `$HOME/dead.letter`.
escape = `char`	Controls which character precedes an input mode (tilde) command. This command takes effect with the next message sent. By default, this variable is set to the tilde.
header	Displays the header summary when entering `mailx`. By default, this variable is set. To disable it, `unset` the variable or `set` the *noheader* variable.

Table 7-4. *Control Variables in Mailx (continued)*

Variable	Function
hold	Causes any message that is read but not deleted to be kept in the mailbox instead of being moved to the mbox file. By default, this feature is not set.
ignore	Refuses interruptions during message creation. This is the same as invoking mailx with the -i option. By default, this variable is not set.
keepsave	Causes mailx to keep the message until you explicitly delete it. Normally, once you save a message, mailx automatically deletes it. The default is *nokeepsave*.
metoo	Permits you to send messages to yourself. Those who use the Reply command set this variable. Reply sends a response message to all users, including you, who received a certain message. Default is nometoo, which excludes you from the list of recipients of any messages you send.
page	Inserts a form feed (CTRL-L) after each message copied into the pipe command; for example, if you send more than one message to lp via the pipe command, each message begins on a new printer page.
PAGER=cmnd	Use the specified shell command cmnd as a filter to paginate messages displayed using the print or type commands. By default, *cmnd* is more. This variable has no effect if the variable *crt* is not set to a value.
prompt=string	Changes the mailx command prompt to a string that you prefer. By default, this variable is set to a question mark (?). My preference is MAIL>.
screen=number	Defines the number of headers that make up a page in the header summary. The h + and h - commands increment and decrement through

Table 7-4. Control Variables in Mailx (continued)

Variable	Function
	the headers by this number. By default, this value is unset and 20 headers are displayed on each page.
SHELL=cmnd	Defines the desired shell if any command requesting a shell (for example, ! or sh) is executed. By default, mailx uses the value from your *SHELL* environmental variable.
VISUAL=cmnd	Defines the editor that the ~v command uses. By default this variable is set to vi.

Part of a .mailrc file follows:

```
set crt=22 cmd=/usr/bin/more
set askcc hold page PAGER=/usr/bin/more
set prompt= "MAIL>" SHELL=/bin/csh
```

As you can see from this listing, you may assign more than one variable for any single set command. If you want to see what variables are set for your e-mail environment, use the set command with no arguments while you are in mailx command mode.

If you are an administrator for a system, you may wish to create a global e-mail start-up file to define certain general characteristics for all users. This global file is located in /usr/lib/mail/mailrc.

Mailx also provides a way to define groups of users to receive messages. For example, if you are a project manager with five people in your department, you will probably want to regularly route messages to all five people. Instead of repeatedly listing each of these users for each message, group them under an e-mail *alias*.

An alias is a unique string that identifies a list of users. Specifying an alias as the destination routes the message to all users defined for the alias. The users are substituted when you specify the alias as a recipient of a message.

For example, suppose you have an alias *dept* that includes Mary, John, Mike, Laurie, and Dave. The electronic mail facility interprets the command

```
$ mailx dept ↵
```

to mean:

```
$ mailx mary john mike laurie dave ↵
```

Declare aliases in your `.mailrc` file. Some sample aliases follow:

```
alias mookie matthew
alias jack jam
alias everyone jack bart julie justin nina alison
```

The first two aliases specify an alternative way to address a single user. The last alias provides a way to specify a list of users (message recipients) with a single alias, *everyone.*

You may designate aliases not only when sending a message, but also when forwarding a message or creating the carbon copy list or the blind copy list for a message.

CRON: PERIODIC EXECUTION OF TASKS

`Cron`, which is usually started when the system is booted, is used to automatically schedule tasks for execution on a periodic basis. These tasks usually include nightly system backup and periodic purging of the files in `/tmp` and `/usr/tmp`.

You may use `cron` to execute tasks by creating a crontab file, a file containing commands for `cron` to execute. A crontab file consists of a series of lines, each containing the following six fields separated either by spaces or tabs:

```
minute hour day month weekday command
```

where

minute   is the minute or minutes of the particular hour on which the command is to execute (0 through 59).

hour   is the hour or hours of the particular day on which the command is to execute (0 through 23).

day   is the particular day or days of the month on which the command is to execute (1 through 31). This field is used to specify certain days in addition to the weekday field.

month   is the month or months in which the command is to execute
(1 through 12).

weekday   is the day or days of the week on which the command is to
execute (0 through 6, where 0 is Sunday and 6 is Saturday).
This field can be used to specify certain days in addition to
the day field.

command   is the command to execute. All programs and files should be
specified using their full pathnames; don't expect cron to use your
value for the *PATH* shell variable.

You can format each field (except *command*) in any of the following ways:

❑ As a single number (for example, 7)

❑ As two numbers separated by a hyphen (for example, 1-5) to indicate a
range of numbers

❑ As a list of numbers separated by commas (for example, 1,8,12) to indicate
a set of specific numbers

❑ As an asterisk (*) to indicate all numbers within the range of a field

The following is an example of a crontab file:

```
20 5 * * * find /tmp /usr/tmp -mtime +5 -exec rm {} \; 2>/dev/null
15 20-8 * * 1-5 ps -ef
1 0 * * 1-5 banner "Good Morning!" | /bin/mail usera
```

The first line tells cron to execute find(1) each day at 5:20 a.m. The find
command causes the removal of any files more than five days old from the
/tmp and /usr/tmp directories. This command redirects stderr to /dev/null,
preventing errors from being reported. (See Chapter 9 for more on find.)

Cron executes the second line hourly from 8:15 p.m. until 8:15 a.m. Monday
through Friday. Because of the weekday restriction, the status is reported
only on Monday from 12:15 a.m. until 8:15 a.m. and on Friday from 8:15
p.m. until 11:15 p.m. When this line executes, the current system status is
reported.

Cron executes the last line each morning at 12:01 a.m. to mail a banner(1)
message to usera. Banner generates a large-lettered poster containing the
string you request—in this case, *Good Morning!*.

All information that a task writes to standard output (stdout) or standard error (stderr), such as the `ps` report in the second line of the example, is routed by `cron` to the e-mail mailbox of the user requesting the command. This user may then view the information with `mailx`(*1*).

`Cron` tasks execute as the user that requested the task (for example, if you are user Steve, `cron` executes the tasks you request as Steve), and all permissions and restrictions associated with the user are enforced. `Cron` executes these tasks using the Bourne shell and assigns values to the shell variables *HOME*, *SHELL* (`/bin/sh`), and *PATH* (`/bin:/usr/bin`) for the task to inherit. `Cron` executes tasks from the requesting user's home directory.

To request `cron` to execute a set of tasks, create a crontab file and register the commands in this file with `cron` via the `crontab`(*1*) command. To register the commands, type

```
$ crontab cfile ⏎
```

where *cfile* is the name of the file containing the `cron` tasks. `Crontab` copies your crontab file into the directory `/usr/spool/cron/crontabs` and names the file with your account name; if your account name is demo, your crontab file is `/usr/spool/cron/crontabs/demo`. Each time the system is rebooted and `cron` starts, it checks this directory for all crontab files containing the tasks it must execute.

The crontab command may respond with this:

```
crontab: you are not authorized to use cron. Sorry.
```

If so, request that your system administrator either remove your account name from the `cron.deny` file or add your account name to the `cron.allow` file. Both files reside in `/usr/lib/cron`. These files control user access to `cron`.

To obtain a list of the tasks you requested `cron` to execute, use:

```
$ crontab -l ⏎
```

To stop `cron` from executing your tasks, execute the following:

```
$ crontab -r ⏎
```

CALENDAR: KEEPING TRACK OF APPOINTMENTS

One command that your system administrator may request `cron` to execute daily is this:

```
calendar -
```

With the - option, `calendar`(1) searches each user's home directory for the file `calendar`. When a `calendar` file is found, its contents are scanned for any entries containing today's or tomorrow's date and `calendar` mails these entries to that user.

You can execute `calendar` without the - option to process your `$HOME/calendar` file; `calendar` reports via stdout any lines containing today's or tomorrow's date.

On Friday, `calendar` includes Saturday, Sunday, and Monday in the tomorrow scan. `Calendar` does not recognize any holidays.

A portion of a sample calendar file for 1989 is shown below:

```
Dec 5 : Dad's Birthday (call him)
12/5 : Judy's Birthday (call her)
December 18: Get skis waxed for trip
12/29: Mom's Birthday (call her)
12/31: New Year's Party at Scott's house
1/1: Stay home - watch football.
Jan 15 - Leave for ski trip to Vail
```

On Friday, December 15, and Monday, December 18, `calendar` reports this message:

```
$ calendar ⏎
December 18: Get skis waxed for trip
$ _
```

On Friday, December 29, calendar reports the following messages:

```
$ calendar ⏎
12/29: Mom's Birthday (call her)
12/31: New Year's Party at Scott's house
1/1: Stay home - watch football.
$ _
```

If you want to see your calendar for today, you can execute the `calendar` command at any time without command arguments, and the output is displayed on your terminal. Place this command into your `.profile` or `.login` file if you want to see your calendar each time you log in.

AT: EXECUTE A TASK AT ANOTHER TIME

Whereas `cron` is used to execute a command on a periodic basis, usually when the system is not busy, `at` executes a series of tasks at a specific time. Once the tasks are completed, they are not executed again unless you request them.

Use the following syntax to execute `at`:

```
$ at time date increment  ↵
```

Specify `at` commands via stdin. You may do so in either of these ways:

❑ Create a file containing the commands to execute and redirect the file into the `at` command (for example, `at <file`).

❑ Execute `at` and enter the tasks from the keyboard, one line per command, terminating the list of commands with a CTRL-D.

The *time* argument may contain one, two, or four digits (9 for 9 a.m.; 21 for 9 p.m.; 1135 for 11:35 a.m.), or two numbers separated by a colon (12:15). You may append *time* with a.m. or p.m.; if not, *time* uses a 24-hour clock. The special time keywords *noon*, *midnight*, and *now* are also acceptable. If you do not specify a time, `at` assumes *now*.

The *date* argument may contain either the month and day (May 9) or the month and day followed by a comma and the year (January 19, 1991). The month may be abbreviated to the first three letters of the month's name. The date may also be specified by the day of the week (Thursday); the day of the week may be abbreviated to the first three letters of the day's name. You may use special date keywords *today* and *tomorrow*. If a date is not specified, either *today* or *tomorrow* is the default, depending on whether the time specified is before (tomorrow) or after (today) the current time.

Increment provides a way to specify relative time and has the form *+ n units*, where *units* is minute, hour, day, week, month, or year. Either the singular or the plural of these keywords is permissible. For example, `now + 3 weeks` indicates 21 days from the current time and date. If not specified, no increment is assumed.

Here are some example times you can use with at:

```
Noon Mar 25
3 pm February 12, 1991
1600 Tomorrow
2359              (11:59 p.m. today)
now + 2 days      (exactly 48 hours from now)
```

When at is invoked with a set of commands to execute, a job number and the time and date for the execution are displayed as follows:

```
job 629782740.a at Fri Dec 15 22:39:00 1989
```

To list the jobs at is scheduled to execute for you:

```
$ at -l ⏎
```

To prevent at from executing a specific job, type

```
$ at -r job_number ⏎
```

where *job_number* is the job number as returned either by at -l or when the at job was scheduled.

An at job automatically sends all stdout and stderr output to your e-mail mailbox. All at commands execute using the Bourne shell. When you submit an at job, both the currently defined shell variables and the current directory are remembered. When at executes the job, these shell variables are restored and at executes the commands from the remembered directory.

The at command may return this error message:

```
at: you are not authorized to use at. Sorry.
```

If so, request that your system administrator either remove your account name from the at.deny file or add your account name to the at.allow file. Both files reside in /usr/lib/cron and control user access to at.

YOU MADE IT!

Congratulations. You've just finished Part II of this book. Now you should be not only well versed in UNIX, but almost comfortable with it.

I hedged with the word *almost* because most users of a new operating system never feel entirely comfortable with the operating system after just reading about it. You have to practice!

Take time now to practice. When you think you are ready, come back and read Part III.

Part III

UNIX, Quicker!

The difference between the average user of an operating system and an advanced user is just this: Do you know how to solve your problem in the shortest amount of time?

This part of the book contains additional information for two topics, vi and shell programming. It shows you ways to use UNIX to accomplish your tasks quickly.

You could skimp on your UNIX education and skip this whole part of the book; however, do you want to know how to type a paragraph in vi without pressing ENTER after each line? Do you want to know how to execute a set of commands for each file in your working directory?

Then keep reading....

Chapter 8

Increasing Your vi Editing Speed

By now you should be proficient with the vi commands discussed in Chapter 4. It's time to show you some of the shortcuts and tricks available with vi.

BUFFERS

When you delete or yank sections of text, vi places the text into a *buffer*. Vi provides 35 buffers—26 named buffers and nine numbered buffers.

The number of named buffers is derived from the number of characters in the alphabet. To place a section of text into a named buffer, preface the yank or delete command with a double quote (") and an uppercase or low-ercase letter indicating the buffer's name.

The buffers named by a lowercase letter are the same as the buffers named by an uppercase letter; however, referencing a buffer by its lowercase name *replaces* the contents of the buffer and referencing a buffer by its uppercase name *appends* to the contents of the buffer.

For example, to delete five lines from your file and place these lines into buffer *r*, type "r5dd. The lowercase letter is the buffer's name. To delete two more lines and append them to this buffer, type "R2dd.

To copy text from a named buffer into your file after the cursor, preface the p or P (put) command with a double quote and the lowercase letter naming the buffer containing the text (for example, "rp). To copy the contents of a named buffer into the file before the cursor, preface the P (put) command with the double quote and lowercase letter.

You can reuse a named buffer by deleting or yanking another section of text into a named buffer that was already storing information. But be careful; this overwrites and loses the old information.

Let's run through a quick example using named buffers. For this example, begin editing the following file:

```
The contents of this file are about to be arranged
in a manner which is more consistent with the
ordered into English sentences.  Once the re-
ordering has taken place, you will be able to use

the named buffers effectively.
Before the message can be read, it must be re-
text message contained in this file.
~
~
~
~
~
~
                                              ○
```

Let's use named buffers to reorder the sentences in the file.

Step 1.   Move to the third line of the file. To delete lines 3 and 4 of this file
and store them in buffer *a*, type "a2dd. The screen now displays this:

```
The contents of this file are about to be arranged
in a manner which is more consistent with the

_
the named buffers effectively.
Before the message can be read, it must be re-
text message contained in this file.
~
~
~
~
~
~
~
```

Step 2.   Delete the last line of the file and store it into buffer *b*. Move the
cursor to the last line and type "bdd:

```
The contents of this file are about to be arranged
in a manner which is more consistent with the

the named buffers effectively.
Before the message can be read, it must be re-
~
~
~
~
~
~
~
~
~
```

Step 3.   Insert the contents of buffer *a* into the file after the cursor, using "ap:

```
The contents of this file are about to be arranged
in a manner which is more consistent with the

the named buffers effectively.
Before the message can be read, it must be re-
ordered into English sentences.  Once the re-
ordering has taken place, you will be able to use
~
~
~
~
~
~
```

Step 4.   Move up to the fourth line and use "add to delete the line and move
it into buffer *a*. Then, insert the contents of buffer *b* after line 2 (move
to line 2 and type "bp). The file now appears as follows:

```
The contents of this file are about to be arranged
in a manner which is more consistent with the
text message contained in this file.
                                        (continued)
```

```
Before the message can be read, it must be re-
ordered into English sentences.  Once the re-
ordering has taken place, you will be able to use

~
~
~
~
~
~
~
```

Step 5. Move to the last line in the file and insert the contents of buffer *a* to complete the reordering of the file:

```
The contents of this file are about to be arranged
in a manner which is more consistent with the
text message contained in this file.

Before the message can be read, it must be re-
ordered into English sentences.  Once the re-
ordering has taken place, you will be able to use
the named buffers effectively.

~
~
~
~
~
~
```

The numbered buffers are organized by vi into a buffer history stack. When you execute a d (delete) command without specifying a named buffer to receive the deleted text (that is, without prefacing the d command with the double quote and lowercase letter), vi puts the text in the buffer history stack.

You can access the item you most recently placed on the buffer history stack by using the p or P command without any prefacing buffer name; this particular buffer history stack location is named the *unnamed buffer*. This form of the p/P (put) command was discussed in Chapter 4.

You can access the slots in the buffer history stack using the buffer names 1 through 9, where 1 is the item most recently placed onto the stack and 9 is the least recently placed item. For example, to retrieve the block of text three deletes ago, type "3p; after the next delete (without naming a buffer), this block of text is retrieved with "4p.

If you use the y (yank) command without a buffer name, the yanked text is placed into buffer 1. Unlike the d (delete) command, the next unnamed yank or delete overwrites this buffer. Unnamed yanks have access only to buffer 1 and do not use buffers 2 through 9.

Once you directly reference any element of the buffer history stack, you cannot simply use the p command to recover the most recently deleted item: you must use "1p. You could say this was a minor defect, or, you could just call it kismet.

Let's go through the same example using only numbered buffers:

```
The contents of this file are about to be arranged
in a manner which is more consistent with the
ordered into English sentences.  Once the re-
ordering has taken place, you will be able to use

the named buffers effectively.
Before the message can be read, it must be re-
text message contained in this file.
~
~
~
~
~
~
```

Step 1. Move to the third line and type 2dd. The screen now displays this:

```
The contents of this file are about to be arranged
in a manner which is more consistent with the

_
the named buffers effectively.
Before the message can be read, it must be re-
```
(continued)

```
text message contained in this file.
~
~
~
~
~
~
~
~
```

Step 2. Move the cursor to the last line and delete the line with dd:

```
The contents of this file are about to be arranged
in a manner which is more consistent with the

the named buffers effectively.
Before the message can be read, it must be re-
~
~
~
~
~
~
~
~
```

Step 3. To insert the two lines of text that you first deleted from the file,
use the command "2p:

```
The contents of this file are about to be arranged
in a manner which is more consistent with the

the named buffers effectively.
Before the message can be read, it must be re-
ordered into English sentences.  Once the re-
ordering has taken place, you will be able to use
~
~
```

(continued)

```
~
~
~
~
~
```

Step 4. Move up to the fourth line and delete the line. (Pop quiz time: What command do you use?) Then insert the text you deleted in step 2 following line 2 using the command "2p:

```
The contents of this file are about to be arranged
in a manner which is more consistent with the
text message contained in this file.

Before the message can be read, it must be re-
ordered into English sentences.  Once the re-
ordering has taken place, you will be able to use
~
~
~
~
~
~
~
```

Step 5. Move to the last line in the file and use "1p to insert the most recently deleted line to complete the reordering of the file:

```
The contents of this file are about to be arranged
in a manner which is more consistent with the
text message contained in this file.

Before the message can be read, it must be re-
ordered into English sentences.  Once the re-
ordering has taken place, you will be able to use
the named buffers effectively.
~
~
~
~                                        (continued)
```

```
~

~
```

Some final notes about buffers:

❏ When vi starts, all buffers are empty.

❏ If you request a new file for editing without leaving vi (that is, you use the
    :e command to request the new file), you lose the contents of the num-
    bered buffers but retain the contents of the 26 named buffers. If you want
    to move text from one file to another, use named buffers to provide
    intermediate storage.

❏ When you exit vi, you lose the contents of all buffers.

MARKERS

As discussed in Chapter 4, vi provides movement and certain editing operations based on objects. Some vi objects already discussed include words,
sentences, and paragraphs.

You may find that movement and editing based on these objects is just not
convenient enough. For example, if you have a long document and want to
move text from the middle of two chapters to the middle of a third, vi
movement based on a word, line or paragraph can be inconvenient;
movement based on text search also may take too long.

It's time to introduce another object, the *marker*. A marker is similar to a
bookmark; it identifies a special location in the file.

For example, the following screen shows a section of text from a long file:

```
The single quotes surround the alias value to
prevent the C shell from interpreting the *; the
backslash precedes the ! to prevent the shell from
interpreting the request as a history
substitution.

The fourth alias creates the stop command to kill
all programs specified as arguments to the command
```
                                                    (continued)

```
For example, stop 8400 performs the command kill
-9 8400.

The fifth alias simplifies the alias command.

The final alias causes the rm command to move
```

Let's say that this text is somewhere in the middle of the file and you just remembered that you need to change some text near the top of the file. To remember your place, put a marker in the file at the current cursor position so you can quickly return.

Vi provides 26 markers for your use. These markers are named (if you can call it that) by the lowercase letters a through z. Although markers have the same names as buffers, the two items are entirely unrelated.

To place a marker, press m and the letter naming your marker. For example, type mw to place the marker named *w* at the cursor position. When you place a marker, vi does not indicate the marker's position or even that the marker was inserted. After using vi for a while, you will accept a marker's existence as a matter of faith.

Now you can move to the top of the file and do your editing. To return to the location for marker *w*, press `w (a single grave followed by the marker's name); vi immediately returns to the location where you placed the marker. In general, `n indicates the position for marker *n*.

You also can use a marker to delimit an object for editing. The object is formed by using the cursor position for one end point and a marker's location for the other (regardless of whether the marker's position is before or after the cursor). Using the above sample screen again, let's delete all text between the word *fourth* (in the seventh line) and the word *alias* in the last line:

Step 1. Move the cursor to the first character of *alias* in the last line:

```
The single quotes surround the alias value to
prevent the C Shell from interpreting the *; the
backslash precedes the ! to prevent the shell from
interpreting the request as a history
substitution.
                                        (continued)
```

```
The fourth alias creates the stop command to kill
all programs specified as arguments to the command
For example, stop 8400 performs the command kill
-9 8400.

The fifth alias simplifies the alias command.

The final alias causes the rm command to move
```

Step 2. Mark this location with marker *h*, using the command mh.

Step 3. Now move to the first character of the word *fourth* in the seventh line:

```
The single quotes surround the alias value to
prevent the C shell from interpreting the *; the
backslash precedes the ! to prevent the shell from
interpreting the request as a history
substitution.

The fourth alias creates the stop command to kill
all programs specified as arguments to the command
For example, stop 8400 performs the command kill
-9 8400.

The fifth alias simplifies the alias command.

The final alias causes the rm command to move
```

Step 4. To perform the deletion, press d`h. The text between the words *fourth* and *alias* is immediately removed and the file now appears like this:

```
The single quotes surround the alias value to
prevent the C shell from interpreting the *; the
backslash precedes the ! to prevent the shell from
interpreting the request as a history
substitution.
```

(continued)

```
The alias causes the rm command to move
files to the /tmp directory.  This alias provides
a primitive method for preventing you from
unintentionally deleting files.

You can create a command that has the same
sequence of characters as a regular UNIX command.
To use the command, instead of the alias, precede
```

By the way, marker *w*, the marker you placed earlier, is still where you placed it. Press `w and the cursor moves to the end of the current line; a marker retains its character position in the file until you exit vi, begin to edit another file, or delete the character anchoring the marker.

You may use markers to specify an object to delete, change, or yank. You may move a marker by reusing it with the m (marker) command; for example, using mw again at a different location in the file causes vi to lose the old marker location and remember the new one.

You also can reference the line in which the marker appears by specifying a single quote followed by the marker's name. The usefulness of this reference is shown later in this chapter.

A QUICK REVIEW

Table 8-1 presents a quick review of the vi commands and features learned thus far in this chapter.

Table 8-1. Quick Review

vi Command	Feature
"*name*	Named buffers. When used with the y (yank) and d (delete) commands, *name* is either a lowercase letter (replacing the contents of the buffer) or an uppercase letter (appending to the contents of the buffer). When used with the p (put) command, *name* is always a lowercase letter or a number (to reference a numbered buffer). Use buffers to move or copy text within the file.

Table 8-1. Quick Review (continued)

vi Command	Features
m*name*	Place a marker (named *name*) at the cursor position.
`` `name ``	*Name* is a lowercase letter naming the marker created using m*name*. Once a marker is placed, use `` `name `` to jump to the location of marker *name*. It can be used to specify an object for the d (delete), y (yank), and c (change) commands.
'*name*	Reference the beginning of the line in which the marker *name* has been created.

A LITTLE EX ...

As I mentioned at the end of Chapter 4, vi is based on the ex(1) editor. Ex, although line-oriented, is very powerful, and it provides features that are not available in vi's full-screen mode. To perform an ex editor command from vi command mode, press the colon and enter the command. The command executes when you press ENTER.

Subsequent sections describe some of the available ex features.

Editing Multiple Files

As discussed in Chapter 4, you can begin editing another file from within vi by using the :e command. Specified without any arguments, the command causes vi to reedit the current file. If you specify another filename as an argument to this command, vi begins editing the specified file.

Another way to edit multiple files within vi is to specify a list of files to edit on the vi command line. For example, you can edit all files in the current directory that end with *.txt* by entering the following:

```
$ vi *.txt ↵
```

If you have three files with the *.txt* suffix in the current directory, vi begins editing the first file in the list. The * wildcard is expanded by the shell in alphabetical order.

Make changes to the first file. Save it using the :w command. To begin editing the next file, enter :n. Edit that file and save it. To move to the final file, enter :n. Edit this file and save it. Entering :n again, since this was the last file in the list, causes vi to display this message:

```
No more files to edit.
```

Enter :q to stop editing.

At any time while you are editing a list of files, you can begin editing from the first file in the list by entering :rew (rewind).

If you make a change to the current file and want to edit another file without saving the change, vi displays a message indicating that you should save the file before executing the requested command. If you don't want to save the file, you must enter a different form of the requested command. Append an exclamation point to the :q, :n, :e, or :rew command (for example, :n!) to execute the command, regardless of whether you have saved the changes to the current file.

While you edit a list of files, you can edit another file that may or may not be in the list by using the :e command. Once you have finished editing this file, use the command :n to continue editing the files in the original list.

Once you are in vi, to see the list of files you are editing, enter the :args command. The specific file you are editing is enclosed in brackets ([]). For example, if you use this command to start vi

```
$ vi july.doc aug.doc sept.doc ⏎
```

executing the :args command returns this:

```
[july.doc] aug.doc sept.doc
```

You cannot create a list of files to edit from within vi.

Regular Expressions

Earlier, when I discussed the / and ? search commands, I omitted some powerful information to protect you from mental overload.

In the discussion of the possible search strings, I mentioned only characters and not *search patterns*. A search pattern is similar to a shell wildcard pattern except much more complicated. These search patterns, called *regular expressions*, are used not only with the editors vi and ex, but also with grep, sed(1), and awk(1).

As complicated as regular expressions (REs) are, learning their power and how to use them is one of the quickest ways to unlock some of the power of UNIX. REs are documented in the reference manual entry for either regexp(5) or ex(1), depending on how your documentation is organized.

This book will not discuss all possible REs. Certain REs are exotic and are not used often enough to warrant space in this book. However, learning some of the power of REs is important.

An RE is composed of text characters and special characters called *metacharacters* (which is another word I can't find in my dictionary; who makes these words up?). Text characters are matched identically with the text being searched; metacharacters provide the mechanism for pattern searches. REs can be used with both the / and ? search commands.

Two important metacharacters are ^ and $, which indicate the beginning of a line and the end of a line, respectively. For example, to search forward through your file for the next line that begins with *The*, the search command is:

    /^The

To search forward for the next line ending with an exclamation point, use the search command:

    /!$

The ^ is a metacharacter if no characters precede it in the search string; otherwise, it is considered to be just another character. The $ is a metacharacter if no characters follow it in the search string.

If you want to search for any line ending with a period, use the search string:

    /\.$

The period is preceded by a backslash because the period also is a metacharacter. Preceding a metacharacter with a backslash disables that character's magic properties. (Don't laugh. Magic is discussed later.) The act of preceding any metacharacter with a backslash is called *escaping*.

A period, when not escaped, matches any single character except for the new-line character. For example, to search for the next line containing exactly one character, use the search command:

```
/^.$
```

As with the shell, you can represent a set of characters you want to match by enclosing the set within square brackets. A set can, as with a shell, contain both single characters and ranges of characters. Two characters separated by a minus sign indicate a range containing all characters between the two specified characters. For example, to search for any number in your text file, use the search string:

```
/[0-9]
```

Another way to think of the period metacharacter is as the complete set of all available characters.

The * metacharacter is different from the * shell wildcard. The * metacharacter represents any number (zero or more instances) of the preceding text character or set of characters. For example, to search for any word beginning with a capital letter, use the command:

```
/[A-Z][a-z]*
```

The [a-z]* represents any number of lowercase letters.

When vi scans for a match, the * represents the largest, left-most number of instances that match the preceding text character or set. For example, if you have the string *Ansg28fhalen10*, the RE [0-9][0-9]* matches the *28* and not just the *2*. See Table 8-2 for a few sample REs and their meanings.

Table 8-2. Some Regular Expressions and Their Meanings

Regular Expressions	Meaning
th[eo]se	Matches *these* and *those*.
^[0-9][0-9]* .*$	Matches a number at the beginning of a line containing other characters. Useful for searching for FORTRAN line numbers.
tty[0-9]*	Matches any string beginning with *tty* and ending with zero or more numbers.

Within vi, searching for text strings is not the only reason to use REs. REs also are used with the substitute command.

Substitution

Like most word processors, vi provides a way to search and replace characters in your text without retyping the replacement each time the search pattern is matched. Unlike most word processors, however, vi also provides some extra tricks to make text replacement more sophisticated.

The substitute command's basic form is:

```
:addresss/search RE/replacement text/
```

In this command, *address* is the list of lines on which to operate, *search RE* is any RE, and *replacement text* replaces the characters matched by the RE. For example, to replace the word *interface* with *interact* throughout your document, enter this command:

```
:1,$s/interface/interact/ ⏎
```

Let's examine this example for a moment. The 1,$ preceding the s command specifies all lines in the document from the first line through the last line of the document. (The $ in an address represents the last line in the document.) The substitution is straightforward: *interact* replaces *interface*.

The substitute command, however, normally operates only on the first occurrence of the search RE in each line checked. To replace every occurrence of the search RE with replacement text in each line specified by the address requires the g (global) option at the end of the command:

```
:1,$s/interface/interact/g ⏎
```

On completion, the substitute command displays on the status line the number of replacements made.

You can specify an address string using any of the constructs listed in Table 8-3.

Specifying a single address (for example, .+5) causes the substitute command to operate only on that line. To specify a range of lines, specify two address fields separated by a comma (for example, 1,$).

Table 8-3. Constructs for Specifying an Address String

Address	Meaning
n	The *n*th line in the file.
$	The last line in the file.
.	The current line in the file.
.+*n*	The *n*th line after the current line.
.-*n*	The *n*th line before the current line.
%	All lines in the file. The same as 1,$.
/RE/	Search forward for a line containing the expression *RE*. The number of that line is used as an address.
?RE?	Search backward for a line containing the expression *RE*. The number of that line is used as an address.
`m	The line in the file containing the specified marker *m*. The character preceding the marker is a single quote, not a grave.

Another way to perform the same substitution is this command:

```
:%s/interface/interact/g ⏎
```

Another example: To restrict the above substitution so that it occurs only between the next line containing the word *START* and the subsequent line containing the word *END*, use this substitution command:

```
:/START/,/END/s/interface/interact/g ⏎
```

Another ex command to use with substitution is :g (global search), which has the following syntax:

```
:g/search RE/command
```

This command searches the file and reports which lines contain the search RE. These line numbers are then used as addresses for the command, which could be the substitute command. For example, to perform the above substitution only on lines containing the word *HERE*, you could use the :g command as follows:

```
:g/HERE/s/interface/interact/
```

Some options for the substitute command can be found in Table 8-4.

Table 8-4. Options for the Substitution Command

Option	Function
c	Confirm each substitution before making it.
r	Execute the previous substitution again for a different address without specifying the search RE or replacement text again. The normal syntax for this command is :*address*s**r**.
p	Display each line after the substitution is made to it.

NOTE: If you need to use / as part of the search RE or replacement text, precede it by a backslash (\) to prevent the substitution command from using that / as a command delimiter.

Let's try a tricky example. Suppose you create a document containing some numbers that you know are wrong. You want to get rid of your false numbers and replace each of these numbers with a pound sign (#). To do this, use an RE for the search RE, as follows:

```
:%s/[0-9]/#/g ⏎
```

Now let's get very tricky. Suppose you wanted to include part of the text matched by search RE in your replacement text. With vi, although it isn't simple, you can do it!

Let's say you have a file containing a list of the filenames for all of your documents, such as the following:

```
october.doc
november.doc1
november.doc2
december.doc
july.doc
may1.doc
may22.doc
february.numbers
~
~
~
~
~
~
```

You want to change this file into a shell script that will change the permissions for these files, permitting you to read from and write to them, and providing read-only permission for all other users. Edit the file and execute the following substitution command:

```
:%s/^\(.*\)$/chmod 644 \1/ ⏎
```

Dissecting this command reveals some interesting substitution features. The RE `^\(.*\)$` performs the same search as the RE `^.*$`; the pair of escaped parentheses indicate that the text matched by the enclosed subexpression should be retained for use in replacement text. The text matched by `.*` is then placed in the location reserved by `\1` in replacement text.

Your file now looks like this:

```
chmod 644 october.doc
chmod 644 november.doc1
chmod 644 november.doc2
chmod 644 december.doc
chmod 644 july.doc
chmod 644 may1.doc
chmod 644 may22.doc
chmod 644 february.numbers
~
~
~                                        (continued)
```

```
    ~
    ~
    ~
 8 substitutions
```

In general, you can specify up to nine subexpressions, numbered from left to right, 1 through 9, within a search RE. You can include the text matching these subexpressions in replacement text. To reserve a place in replacement text for this text, place a backslash followed by the subexpression number.

Here's another example: To reverse the order of the words in each line, enter this command:

```
:%s/^\(.*\) \(.*\) \(.*\)$/\3 \2 \1/ ⏎
```

The file now looks like this:

```
october.doc 644 chmod
november.doc1 644 chmod
november.doc2 644 chmod
december.doc 644 chmod
july.doc 644 chmod
may1.doc 644 chmod
may22.doc 644 chmod
february.numbers 644 chmod
    ~
    ~
    ~
    ~
    ~
    ~
 8 substitutions
```

Analyze this command before continuing, paying particular attention to how each \(.*\) subexpression translated into one of the place holders (for example, \3) in the replacement text. This particular command didn't do anything to improve the file, but it did demonstrate some of the power of REs and subexpressions in editing. One more feature I have not shown: A subexpression can be referenced more than once in replacement text. For example, you may use the string "\3 \3" within the replacement text.

Spend some time getting comfortable with REs and subexpressions before continuing with the next section.

MORE VI/EX COMMANDS

This section is the catch-all for any useful vi commands I have not already discussed. All commands discussed in this section should be performed from vi command mode.

For example, while you are editing, press CTRL-G, and vi displays the following information: the name of the file, whether the file has unsaved modifications, whether the file is read-only, the line number (the line the cursor is on), the total number of lines in the work area, and the cursor's relative location within the work area, expressed as a percentage. A sample line could be this:

```
"file12" [Modified] line 24 of 240 --10%--
```

Another easy one: If you want to redraw your screen (if, for example, a background program routes messages to your screen while you are editing), press CTRL-L.

One final simple command: While in text entry mode, if you want to add a control character to your file, precede the control character with CTRL-V. The CTRL-V echoes only until you press the desired control character. Then the CTRL-V is removed and the control character is displayed as the two-character sequence containing ^ followed by another character.

If you want to merge another file into the work area, use the :r command. The syntax for this command is:

```
:liner filename
```

In this command, *line* has the same format as *address* in the substitute command and is optional. If *line* is not specified, the contents of the file *filename* are inserted beginning at the line following the cursor's position. If *line* is specified, the contents of *filename* are inserted into the work area beginning at the line following *line*. If *line* is 0, insertion begins at the beginning of the work area. You should always specify a filename.

If you want to insert the results of a UNIX command into your work area, use a variant of the :r command:

```
:liner !command ⏎
```

In this command, *line* has the same meaning as when you insert from a file. However, all results that *command* writes to stdout are inserted into your work area at the location specified (depending on *line*, as discussed above). When you specify *command*, ex/vi expands the percent sign (%) to the name of the file you are editing.

NOTE: Using % to indicate the name of the file you are editing is different from using it to specify the address including all lines in the file. Vi interprets each use of the % according to the context.

For example, most UNIX systems include the spell(*1*) command to check files for spelling errors. To append the list of spelling errors to your work area, save the file using :w and enter the command:

```
:$r !spell % ⏎
```

REMINDER: The dollar sign indicates the last line in your work area.

In the event that your system crashes (as in a power failure) while you are editing a file, vi may preserve your most recent changes even if you have not saved them yourself. Once your system is restarted, you may find that your file does not contain the most recent changes you made. If so, run the following command before you make any changes to the file:

```
:rec ⏎
```

This command attempts to recover the changes you last made to the file before the system crashed. If nothing happens, then just sigh and remember to save your work more often.

While in vi, you might want to jump into a shell to examine other files, run programs, or whatever. To create a temporary shell, enter the :shell command. Within this shell, you can execute any command (similar to your login shell). To continue editing your file, type

```
$ exit ⏎
```

and vi instructs you to press any key to continue, which you should do. If you want to execute only a single shell command, enter:

```
:!command ⏎
```

As mentioned for the :r command, vi expands the % into the name of the file you are editing. So if you want to run spell on this file (without having the results inserted into the work area), save the file and then do this:

```
:!spell % ⏎
```

Remember, if you don't save the contents of your work area to the file, the above command operates on the (possibly) old contents of the file. Any changes you have not saved are not considered, since these changes are not part of the file.

To check the spelling of the text in your work area, enter:

```
:w !spell ↵
```

This command is similar to :r !, except that it writes the contents of the work area to stdin for the specified command. You may route only a portion of the file by specifying an address or range of addresses before the *w* in the command. For example, to print all text between the cursor and the marker *n*, enter:

```
:.,'nw !lp ↵
```

Vi remembers the last shell command you entered. To execute it again, enter the :!! command.

Suppose you (or, as the ads say, someone you love) creates a program called adj to justify text to a certain margin width. This program reads blocks of text from stdin, justifies it, and returns the results to stdout.

How can you use this program to justify the margins of a couple of paragraphs in your file? Use the following file for an example:

```
The contents of this file are
about to be arranged
in a manner which is more
consistent with the
text message contained in the file.

Before the message can be read, it
must be reordered into English sentences.
Once the reordering has
taken place, you will be able to use
the named buffers effectively.
~
~
~
```

Let's use adj to justify the two paragraphs in this file without leaving the editor and without saving the file. Move the cursor to the beginning of the section you want to justify. To justify two paragraphs, the vi object describing two paragraphs is 2}.

Now, type the command !2}adj. Notice as you type this command that the ! does not echo until you specify the 2}, which never echoes. On the status line, vi displays this:

```
  ~
!adj_
```

Press ENTER to execute this command. The specified object is removed from your work area and sent to adj as stdin. All stdout from adj is placed into the work area at the cursor location. If adj only provides left justification for 50-character lines, the following file results:

```
The contents of this file are about to be arranged
in a manner which is more consistent with the
text message contained in the file.

Before the message can be read, it must be re-
ordered into English sentences.  Once the re-
ordering has taken place, you will be able to use
the named buffers effectively.
  ~
  ~
  ~
  ~
  ~
  ~
3 fewer lines
```

The ! command, which is the command just executed, is similar to the d (delete), y (yank), and c (change) commands in that the command always requires an object on which to execute (and !! operates only on the current line). Like the d, c, and y commands, an object can be a word, line, sentence, paragraph, or text bounded by a marker.

Here's another example to provide some idea of the capability of the ! command: UNIX provides a sort(1) utility to read text from stdin, sort it alphabetically, and write the sorted text to stdout. Consider a section of a file containing the following list:

```
The following foods are not considered exotic:

oranges
apples
bananas
sausages
pastrami
grapes
cantaloupe
squash
broccoli
strawberries


Among other cultures, these foods are exotic and
```

To sort this list, move the cursor up one line and place marker *k* at that position, using the command mk. Then, move up to the top of the list and enter the command !'ksort. Before you press ENTER, your screen should appear like this:

```
The following foods are not considered exotic:

oranges
apples
bananas
sausages
pastrami
grapes
cantaloupe
squash
broccoli
strawberries


Among other cultures, these foods are exotic and
!sort_
```

Press ENTER. The lines are removed from the work area and in its place the sorted list appears:

```
The following foods are not considered exotic:

apples
bananas
broccoli
cantaloupe
grapes
oranges
pastrami
sausages
squash
strawberries

Among other cultures, these foods are exotic and
```

Pretty cool, huh? If you improperly enter the command to execute, the specified object is removed from the file, but nothing may be returned. **DON'T PANIC!** All ex/vi editing commands can be reversed with the u (undo) command. In fact, to reverse the sort just performed, press u and watch the file change to the following:

```
The following foods are not considered exotic:

oranges
apples
bananas
sausages
pastrami
grapes
cantaloupe
squash
broccoli
strawberries

Among other cultures, these foods are exotic and
```

By the way, if you want to sort this list and place the result into three columns, use the command !'ksort | pr -3tw50, resulting in this:

```
    The following foods are not considered exotic:

    apples         grapes         sausages
    bananas        oranges        squash
    broccoli       pastrami       strawberries
    cantaloupe

    Among other cultures, these foods are exotic and
    ...
```

This command passes the output from sort to pr(1), and the output from pr(1) is placed back into the file. The pr option -3 specifies three-column output and the -t option specifies that pr should suppress the header it normally prints. The -w50 option causes the output to fit within a page width of 50 characters.

SETTING UP THE VI ENVIRONMENT

Like most word processors, vi provides many options to tailor its environment to your liking.

What kind of configuration can you perform? While in vi, enter the command :set all to view all of the current configuration settings. In general, vi provides at least 40 configuration options that you may set to your liking with the :set command.

Which of these settings are important or useful? The following list explains the effect of setting some of these options. The abbreviation for each command is shown in parentheses:

:set ignorecase (:set ic) — Ignore case distinction for all searches. In other words, searching for FOX is the same as searching for FOx, FoX, Fox, fOX, and so on. To distinguish between uppercase and lowercase letters, use :set noic.

:set magic — Remember, I mentioned earlier that RE metacharacters had magic properties. Normally set, this option enables the RE metacharacters * and . for pattern searches. Use :set nomagic to disable these metacharacters. While disabled, metacharacters become available only by escaping them (preceding them by a backslash).

:set number (:set nu) — When displaying a file, precede each line in the file with its line number. To turn this feature off, use :set nonu. The line numbers are never stored as part of the file.

`:set showmode (:set smd)` — Displays the current editor mode (such as input mode) on the lower right-hand corner of the screen. Use `:set nosmd` to turn this feature off.

`:set showmatch (:set sm)` — Causes `vi` to temporarily jump to the matching parenthesis or bracket in the pair when `)` or `}` is typed in text entry mode. This feature is useful for programmers who are never sure if their parentheses match. Use `:set nosm` to turn off this feature.

`:set warn` — Normally set, this feature displays the warning message "no write since last change" when you attempt either the `:!` or `:shell` commands. Use `:set nowarn` to suppress this message.

`:set wrapscan (:set ws)` — Normally set, this feature permits the search commands `/`, `?`, `n`, and `N` to wrap around to the opposite end of the file and continue the search. Use `:set nows` to stop a search either at the beginning of the file or the end of the file, depending on the direction of the search.

Certain configuration commands optimize `vi` to the type of file you are creating. For example, if you are creating a text document and want to restrict the line length to 72 characters, set the *wrapmargin* configuration option as follows:

```
:set wm=8 ⏎
```

Once you set this option, any word that extends into the last eight characters of a line automatically moves to the beginning of the next line. You need not press ENTER until you are finished with a paragraph; `vi` performs text entry similar to the way most word processors operate.

If the *wrapmargin* is set to 0, the word wrapping feature is disabled and you will need to press ENTER at the end of each line.

If you are developing an outline, you can set several `vi` configuration options to control heading indentation. Setting the *autoindent* (*ai*) option in text entry mode causes `vi` to use the indentation for the previous line to determine the indentation for the next line.

For example, set *autoindent* (`:set ai`) and enter the following line:

```
        I. Getting Started_
```

Press ENTER. The cursor moves to the next line, and `vi` inserts enough spaces or tabs so that the cursor's location is now this:

```
        I. Getting Started
        _
```

Indentation is also related to the *shiftwidth*, which you specify as follows:

```
:set shiftwidth=# ⏎
```

Another way to specify this option is `:set sw=#`. In these commands, # is the number of spaces to shift a line of the file when you use the commands << (shift line left) and >> (shift line right). By default, the *shiftwidth* is eight; for the examples in this section, set the shiftwidth to three.

Continue entering the outline until you have the following:

```
        I. Getting Started
           A. First, Your Manuals
           B. Getting Started with Your System
              1. Where Are You?
              2. Most Other Users
              _
```

You have completed this outline section and want to back up to the previous level of indentation. Pressing BACKSPACE causes the terminal to beep; you cannot back up before the automatic indentation. To decrease the indentation by the current *shiftwidth*, press CTRL-D while in text entry mode. The cursor moves back to:

```
        I. Getting Started
           A. First, Your Manuals
           B. Getting Started with Your System
              1. Where Are You?
              2. Most Other Users
           _
```

Enter the C heading to complete the outline:

```
        I. Getting Started
           A. First, Your Manuals
           B. Getting Started with Your System
              1. Where Are You?
              2. Most Other Users
           C. Some Simple Commands_
```

Press ESCAPE to leave text entry mode and move the cursor to the top of the outline:

```
        I. Getting Started
           A. First, Your Manuals
           B. Getting Started with Your System
              1. Where Are You?
              2. Most Other Users
           C. Some Simple Commands
```

To show the power of the *shiftwidth* feature, type 6<< to shift the six lines three characters to the left:

```
        I. Getting Started
           A. First, Your Manuals
           B. Getting Started with Your System
              1. Where Are You?
              2. Most Other Users
           C. Some Simple Commands
```

You may also specify one or more objects to be shifted by the < and > commands. For example, mark the present position with marker *t* and move to the C heading. Now type >'t and the outline moves to the right by three spaces.

NOTE: Programmers who want to create "pretty" structured code should use the autoindent feature.

The shift commands remove or add blanks or tabs from or to the beginning of each line being shifted; non-white-space characters are never altered by these commands. If *autoindent* is set, white-space characters are added to a line only after you enter text to the line; no white-space characters are ever added to an empty line.

One other configuration setting can control how a file is displayed: *tabstop* (*ts*). To set this variable, use this command:

```
:set ts=#  ⏎
```

In this command, # specifies the number of spaces a tab represents when displaying a file. By default, *tabstop* is eight.

The best setting for your *tabstop* is an integer multiple of the *shiftwidth*. For example, if your *shiftwidth* is set to three, the *tabstop* should be set to three, six, nine, or another multiple of three. Why? Because the *autoindent* option and shift commands insert either spaces or tabs, whichever causes the smallest number of characters to be inserted. If the *tabstop* is a multiple of the *shiftwidth*, automatic indentation always inserts the smallest number of characters into your file.

Many other :set options are available (as shown by the :set all command). For descriptions of these settings, refer to the manpage entries for vi(*1*) and ex(*1*).

The vi Configuration File

Once you determine the configuration settings you like, you won't usually change them. However, entering these settings each time you start vi wastes time.

So ... vi uses the (ta-da!) *vi Configuration File*, which is located in $HOME/.exrc. This file is also known as your exrc file.

When vi starts and before the first file is loaded into the work area, it reads and processes the commands from the exrc file. These commands are always ex commands, although you do not begin them with a colon. For example, to set *autoindent*, a *shiftwidth* of three, the *tabstop* to six, and *magic*, create an exrc file containing the following line:

```
set ai magic sw=3 ts=6
```

As you may have noticed, set options may be combined on a single line, although this is not required. If you want to place comment lines in the exrc file, begin the line with a double quote; vi ignores comment lines.

Mapping the Keyboard

Just placing `set` commands in the `exrc` file is okay, but `vi` provides another really neat configuration feature that you usually initialize with this file: *keyboard mapping*.

Keyboard mapping is performed with the `:map` command. The syntax for the command is as follows:

```
:map key action ⏎
```

In this syntax, *key* is a single character, an escape or control character sequence, or the sequence *#n*, where *n* is the number corresponding to one of your terminal's function keys. The *action* argument is the set of instructions to perform when the specified key is pressed.

For example, to map function key 1 on your keyboard to enter the command `:w!`, enter this command:

```
:map #1 :w!^V^M ⏎
```

Once this mapping is executed, pressing function key 1 while in command mode causes `vi` to execute the `:w!` command. The trailing CTRL-M (^M) represents the ENTER key, without which the `:w!` would only be displayed on the status line, and you would need to press ENTER to execute it. Create the CTRL-M by pressing first CTRL-V and then CTRL-M. The CTRL-V delays interpretation of CTRL-M.

Suppose you want to check the spelling of the text in your file and place the results after your text by pressing the letter S. Enter this command:

```
:map S :w!^V^MG:r !spell %^V^M ⏎
```

Once you have defined it, pressing S causes the following steps to occur: the `:w!^V^M` saves the work area to the file; the `G` moves the cursor to the end of the work area; and the `:r !spell %^V^M` checks the spelling of the contents of the file and reads the results into the work area.

To map ^P (CTRL-P) to print the contents of the work area, use this command:

```
:map ^V^P :%w !1p^V^M ⏎
```

In the above example, ^V is not stored as part of the key sequence; only the ^P is retained.

To remove a keyboard map entry, use the `:unmap` command:

```
:unmap key ⏎
```

Keyboard mapping is usually performed in the `$HOME/.exrc` file. When you place it in the `exrc` file, do not begin the `map` command with a colon.

CHAPTER REVIEW

Table 8-5. Commands for Faster vi Editing

Command	Function
`"`*name*	Named buffers. When used with the `y` and `d` commands, *name* is either a lowercase letter replacing the contents of the buffer or an uppercase letter appending to the contents of the buffer. When used with the `p` command, *name* is always a lowercase letter or the number of a numbered buffer. Use buffers to move or copy text within the file.
`m`*name*	Place a marker (named *name*) at the cursor position.
`` ` ``*name*	*Name* is a lowercase letter naming the marker created with `m`*name*. Once a marker is placed, use `` ` ``*name* to jump to the location of marker *name*. This command can be used to specify an object for the `d` (delete), `y` (yank), or `c` (change) command.
`'`*name*	Reference the beginning of the line in which the marker *name* has been created.
`!`*objcmd*	Execute *cmd*; the work area contents between the current cursor location and the location of the object (*obj*) are passed to *cmd* as stdin; the stdout results replace this section of the work area.
`^G`	Display the file status and the location of the cursor.

Table 8-5. Commands for Faster vi Editing (continued)

Command	Function
^L	Redraw the screen.
^V	Precede any control characters you plan to insert into the file.

Table 8-6. Multiple-File Editing Commands

Command	Function
:n, :n!	Edit the next file in the list.
:rew, :rew!	Reedit the files specified as arguments to vi, starting with the first file in the list.
:args	Show the list of files being edited. The file you are editing is enclosed in brackets.

Table 8-7. Regular Expression Metacharacters

Command	Function
^	Indicates the beginning of a line when used at the beginning of an expression.
$	Indicates the end of a line when used at the end of an expression.
[]	Groups a set or range of characters.
.	Matches any character.
*	Matches zero or more occurrences of the previous character or set of characters.

Table 8-7. Regular Expression Metacharacters (continued)

Command	Function
\(\)	Groups a set of characters and metacharacters into a subexpression. You can reference each sub-expression using a backslash followed by the number of the subexpression numbered from left to right in the expression. For example, \2 is the second subexpression in the expression.
\	When preceding a metacharacter, escapes the metacharacter, making it just a character.

Table 8-8. Substitution

The general syntax for the substitution command is 　:*addr*s/*old*/*new*/*opt* where the elements are defined as follows:	
addr	An address, describing the line or lines on which to operate. The possible forms for this address are *addr* and *addr,addr*. In either form, *addr* is one of these: *n* (the *n*th line in the file) $ (the last line in the file) . (the current line) .+*n* (*n* lines past the current line) .-*n* (*n* lines before the current line) % (all lines; same as 1,$) /RE/ (search forward for the first line containing RE) ?RE? (search backward for the first line containing RE) 'm (the line in the file containing the marker *m*)
old	A regular expression describing the text to substitute.
new	The replacement text.

Table 8-8. Substitution (continued)

`opt`	A set of options that include: g (replace all occurrences in each line) c (confirm each substitution before making it) r (reexecute the previous substitution. Use this option without specifying *old* or *new*) p (display each line after the substitution has been made to it)

Table 8-9. Other vi/ex Commands

Command	Function
`:g/RE/cmd`	Executes the `ex` *cmd* on each line containing text matching the expression *RE. cmd* is usually the substitute command.
`:liner file`	Merges the specified file into the current work area after the specified line. If the specified line is 0, the file is placed before contents of the work area.
`:liner !cmd`	Executes the UNIX *cmd* and places stdout results in the work area after the specified line.
`:rec`	Recovers any changes made but not saved when the system crashed.
`:shell`	Starts a shell based on your *SHELL* environment variable. When you exit the shell, you will be back in `vi`.
`:!cmd`	Executes the UNIX *cmd* without leaving `vi`. The results are not read into your work area.
`:w !cmd`	Executes the UNIX *cmd*, using the contents of the work area as stdin for the command.

Table 8-9. Other vi/ex Commands (continued)

Command	Function
`:set` *opt*	Sets or unsets the `vi` option *opt*. In general, more than 40 options are available with `vi`.
`:map` *key action*	Maps the keyboard keystroke *key* to execute the `vi` *action*. If *key* is a number preceded by #, the number represents the function key pressed to make the *action* occur.
`:unmap` *key*	Removes a keyboard mapping defined with `:map`.

Chapter 9

Shell Programming II

Why learn more about shell programming? Because a shell program is often the shortest distance between a problem and its solution.

Besides providing shell environment configuration, shell scripts are a quick way to perform repetitive tasks. Suppose, for example, you want to edit each document containing spelling errors in a directory. You could, for each file in the directory, execute these commands:

```
$ spell file ⏎
$ vi file ⏎
```

However, this action is too mechanical and requires you to enter these commands for every file in your directory. If you have 25 files with spelling errors in the directory, you will need to enter 50 commands. Shell scripts provide a faster way to perform this operation.

This chapter is separated into two parallel sections: one on Bourne shell programming and one on C shell programming. At the end of this chapter, you should know the important shell commands used to program with either shell.

One caveat, however: For the highest degree of portability between UNIX systems, you should create any shell scripts using Bourne shell commands, not C shell commands. Any temporary scripts can be created with either command set. Scripts you plan to use on more than one UNIX system should always be created using Bourne shell commands.

GENERAL NOTES ABOUT SHELL SCRIPTS

In addition to the general script information provided near the beginning of Chapter 6, you need two more pieces of information:

1. Any shell scripts you create must have execute permission for you to run

them. To add execution permission to a shell script file, use the command

```
$ chmod +x script ↵
```

where *script* is the name of your shell script. For more information about chmod(1), see Chapter 2 of this book or Section 1 of the *UNIX Reference Manual*.

2. If you are running the C shell, you should run the rehash command after you make the script executable. The rehash command was discussed near the end of Chapter 5.

REMINDER: Bourne shell scripts cannot begin with a comment symbol (#) as the first character of the first line. C shell scripts must have a comment character as the first character of the script's first line.

BOURNE SHELL PROGRAMMING

Chapter 6 discussed several Bourne shell programming constructs. The following sections discuss additional constructs that are useful in creating shell scripts.

Shell Arguments and Other Parameters

Like all UNIX programs, shell programs can be written to accept and understand command-line arguments. Each "word" on the command line is numbered from left to right, beginning with the script's name, which is word 0. Shell scripts use *positional parameters* to obtain the values for these words.

For example, in the command

```
$ copy_scr file1 file2 ↵
```

the command copy_scr is word 0, file1 is word 1, and file2 is word 2. If copy_scr is a shell script, then:

$0 contains the string copy_scr
$1 contains the string file1
$2 contains the string file2

You may access only 10 positional parameters, *$0* through *$9*, at a time. If more than nine arguments (the words following the command) are specified, the remaining arguments are placed into a buffer. You may then access the additional arguments via the shell command `shift`, which will be discussed momentarily.

To obtain the count of command-line arguments, use the shell parameter *$#*. The most common use for this parameter is the `test`:

```
if [ $# -gt 0 ]
then
    ... interpret the arguments ...
fi
```

The parameter *$** contains all arguments on the command line; a single space separates the arguments. The value for this parameter does not include any redirection (for example, pipes) specified for the script: only the command's arguments are included.

Most shell scripts you write will use fewer than nine arguments, so the number of positional parameters should be sufficient. If not, you must `shift` the parameters.

When you `shift` the positional parameters, the value in *$2* moves to *$1*, the value in *$3* moves to *$2*, and so on. The value in *$0* (the name of the shell script) is never changed or lost. The first value in the buffer containing all remaining arguments shifts into *$9*. If there are no remaining arguments, an empty string is placed into *$9*. The value that was in *$1* is no longer available.

The value for *$#* decrements after a `shift`, reflecting the number of arguments currently maintained. The value for *$** reflects the removal of the first argument from the list.

Consider the positional parameters as a modified stack, graphically represented by the following diagram:

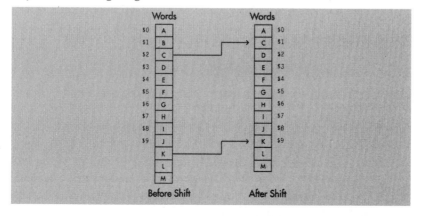

In the above diagram, the command-line words are the letters *A* through *M*. Before the `shift`, the values of the first 10 words (*A* through *J*) are available through the positional parameters. After the `shift`, the positional parameters contain the letters *A* and *C* through *K* (*$5* was *F* and is now *G*).

The syntax for the shift command is

```
shift n
```

where *n* is optional and is the number of arguments to `shift`. If *n* is not specified, then only one `shift` is performed.

Let's create the script `copy_scr`, containing the following:

```
: /bin/sh
echo Prog name: $0
echo First arg: $1
shift
echo Second arg: $1
```

Notice after the `shift` that *$1* is referenced again; after the `shift`, *$1* contains what was the second argument. Remember, the colon command in the first line does nothing except identify the file as a Bourne shell script (instead of a C shell script, which requires that the first line be a comment line). Make the script executable using `chmod(1)`, and then execute it:

```
$ copy_scr file1 file2 ↵
Prog name: copy_scr
First arg: file1
Second arg: file2
$ _
```

So far I've only shown you how to `shift` positional parameters. What if you have a shell variable that contains a list of filenames and you need to `shift` the contents of the variable in this same manner?

You cannot directly do this. However, you can copy the contents of the shell variable to the positional parameters with the command

```
set -- $var
```

where *var* is the name of the variable containing one or more words separated by spaces. The first word in *var* is assigned to *$1*, the second to *$2*, and so on. You can now perform the `shift`. To copy the resulting values back to *var*, use the command:

```
var=$*
```

The `set` command has many more uses, described later in this chapter.

Concatenating Variables to Strings

The values both within shell variables and within shell parameters may be concatenated (joined end to end) to other strings to form new values. For example, suppose you want to create a shell script to access a set of related documents, all of which end with the suffix _doc, but you don't want to specify the suffix each time you access any of the documents. This script might obtain the filename from one of the positional parameters and place it into the variable `file1`. To add the suffix to the value in this variable, you could try:

```
file1=$file1_doc
```

However, the shell interprets this statement as copying the contents of the (possibly nonexistent) variable `file1_doc` into the variable `file1`. To separate the shell variable name from any text concatenated to it, enclose the variable name in braces:

```
file1=${file1}_doc
```

If the document you request is named /usr/tmp/ty1 and this name has been placed into `file1`, the above command changes the value in `file1` to /usr/tmp/ty1_doc.

More Ways to Do Conditional Comparisons

The `if` construct (discussed in Chapter 6) can become unwieldy if you have a condition with several possibilities. To simplify the script, use the `case` command. The `case` construct has the following syntax:

```
case var in
   pattern1) commands1 ;;
   pattern2) commands2 ;;
         .
         .
         .
esac
```

In the above construct, *var* is either a shell variable or a shell parameter; each pattern describes a set of choices that *var's* value equals; and *commands* are the commands executed when *pattern* matches *var's* value. Each pattern is created using regular characters and shell wildcard characters, and each pattern uses the same rules as the shell wildcards (see Chapter 3). The esac (case spelled backward) statement is required to conclude the case construct.

You also should note in this construct that:

❑ Each pattern to match *var* ends with a right parenthesis.

❑ Each group of commands (for a specific pattern) must be terminated with a double semicolon (;;).

Instead of describing a case construct, let's examine one:

```
case $2 in
  +)   echo "Addition requested."
       echo "$1 + $3 = `expr $1 + $3`" ;;

  -)   echo "Subtraction requested."
       echo "$1 - $3 = `expr $1 - $3`" ;;

 \*)   echo "Multiplication requested."
       echo "$1 * $3 = `expr $1 \* $3`" ;;

  /)   echo "Division requested."
       echo "$1 / $3 = `expr $1 / $3`" ;;

  %)   echo "Modulo Arithmetic requested."
       echo "$1 % $3 = `expr $1 % $3`" ;;

  *)   echo "Unknown operation specified.";;
esac
```

This example shows a segment of a shell script to provide simple addition (+), subtraction (-), multiplication (*), division (/), and modulo (%) operations on two arguments. If you place this example into the file math, you can execute it like this:

```
$ math 14 + 12 ↵
Addition requested.
14 + 12 = 26
$ _
```

One other item to notice: the first * pattern is preceded by a backslash and the second is not. The first * in the case example is preceded by a backslash to prevent anything except the character * from matching it. The second one matches all values for $2 but only executes if one of the previous patterns does not match $2 (basically an else construct).

The same segment could have been written (although in a less compact form) using the following if construct:

```
if [ "$2" = "+" ]
then
    echo "Addition requested."
    echo "$1 + $3 = `expr $1 + $3`"
elif [ "$2" = "-" ]
then
    echo "Subtraction requested."
    echo "$1 - $3 = `expr $1 - $3`"
elif [ "$2" = "*" ]
then
    echo "Multiplication requested."
    echo "$1 * $3 = `expr $1 \* $3`"
elif [ "$2" = "/" ]
then
    echo "Division requested."
    echo "$1 / $3 = `expr $1 / $3`"
elif [ "$2" = "%" ]
then
    echo "Modulo Arithmetic requested."
    echo "$1 % $3 = `expr $1 % $3`"
else
    echo "Unknown operation requested."
fi
```

Use the or (|) operator between patterns if you want to execute a single set of commands when either pattern matches the value for *var*. For example, if you want to specify the arithmetic operation in the preceding example using either the arithmetic symbol or a three-character string, change the segment to this:

```
case $2 in
    [Aa][dD][dD] | +)
        echo "Addition requested."
```

```
              echo "$1 + $3 = `expr $1 + $3`" ;;
       [Ss][Uu][Bb] | -)
              echo "Subtraction requested."
              echo "$1 - $3 = `expr $1 - $3`" ;;
       [Mm][Uu][Ll] | \*)
              echo "Multiplication requested."
              echo "$1 * $3 = `expr $1 \* $3`" ;;
       [Dd][Ii][Vv] | /)
              echo "Division requested."
              echo "$1 / $3 = `expr $1 / $3`" ;;
       [Mm][Oo][Dd] | %)
              echo "Modulo Arithmetic requested."
              echo "$1 % $3 = `expr $1 % $3`" ;;
       *)  echo "Unknown operation specified.";;
   esac
```

The | operator separates the pattern possibilities for each selection. The patterns specified above match operation strings that are in uppercase, lowercase, or a combination of uppercase and lowercase. For example, Mod, MOD, mod, and % match the patterns for the modulo operation.

Imagine the above example using if statements.

Looping

One of the most important shell programming features is *looping*. Three Bourne shell looping commands are available: for, while, and until. Each of these commands provides a way to repeat a set of commands.

The general syntax for a looping command is this:

```
loop_control
do
    commands
done
```

The *loop_control* statement is either for, while, or until, and the specific syntax for this statement is based on the particular *loop_control* command chosen. While the *loop_control* statement permits, the commands between the do and done statements are repeatedly executed.

The for command provides a way to perform commands once for each new value assigned to a shell variable. The syntaxes for the for loop are:

```
for variable
do
    commands
done
```

or

```
for variable in list
do
    commands
done
```

In these syntaxes, *variable* is the name for any shell variable. A new value is assigned to *variable* from the contents of *list* if a list has been specified. If *list* is omitted (the first form), *variable* is assigned a value from $* (all positional parameters not shifted).

The *list* value can be a list of strings separated by blanks that you specify, or it can be generated from one or more shell commands. For example:

```
for file1 in `/bin/ls *.doc *.txt`
do
    echo "Copying $file1 ..."
    cp $file1 /tmp/amf
done
```

In this example, the ls command creates a list; the for command assigns each value in this list — one filename at a time — to the variable file1. The commands between do and done then execute (once for each value assigned to file1), copying each file in the list into the directory /tmp/amf. When it reaches the end of the list, the for loop does not repeat.

Since this is a shell script, shell wildcards have the same meaning as if you had specified the wildcard at a shell prompt. In other words, you can write the above example like this:

```
for file1 in *.doc *.txt
do
    echo "Copying $file1 ..."
    cp $file1 /tmp/amf
done
```

In this version, you don't need ls because the shell automatically expands the * wildcard into a file list.

We'll get back to looping after a brief interlude.

Using the `find` Command

One limitation of `ls` is that it cannot generate a usable list when traversing a directory tree, for example to list all files in all directories in the `/usr/lib` directory. The only option available is `-R` (recursive listing), and the resulting output is not readily usable as a list for the `for` command.

To generate a usable list from a directory tree, use `find(1)`, which has the following syntax:

```
find files options
```

In this syntax, *files* are the names of one or more files or directories. If a directory is specified, all files and directories in it are processed. The *options* specify either the criteria for processing a file or directory or the actions that `find` should perform for files and directories matching the specified criteria.

All options are evaluated from left to right. Each file or directory that `find` processes is tested against the options. If an option is not true for the file or directory, `find` stops processing the file and proceeds to the next file.

Table 9-1 lists some useful options for the `find` command.

Table 9-1. Options for the `find` Command

Option	Effect or Use
-print	The most often used option, which sends the name of the file or directory being processed to stdout. Without this option you may not be able to determine which files or directories successfully match the preceding options. In general, specify this option last.
-name *pattern*	Processes the file if *pattern* matches the name of the file, ignoring any directory path preceding the file's name. The pattern can either be a string of characters or a shell wildcard pattern enclosed in single quotes. Without the quotes, the shell interprets the wildcards before `find` gets a chance.

Table 9-1. Options for the `find` *Command (continued)*

Option	Effect or Use
`-type` *x*	Processes the file if the file's type is *x*, where *x* is either f (regular file) or d (directory). Other values for *x* are possible; refer to the manual entry for `find(1)`.
`-size` *n*	Processes the file if the file's size is *n* blocks. A block is 512 bytes. Specifying `-size` +*n* processes the file if it is larger than *n* blocks; specifying `-size` -*n* processes the file if it is smaller than *n* blocks.
`-mtime` *n*	Processes the file if it was modified *n* days ago. See the example following this table. If `-mtime` -*n* is specified, the file is processed if it has been modified in the past *n* days; if `-mtime` +*n* is specified, the file is processed if it has not been modified in the past *n* days.
`-exec` *cmd*	Executes the UNIX command *cmd* for the file or directory being processed. You must terminate *cmd* with a backslash followed by a semicolon (\ ;) to separate the end of *cmd* from any subsequent options. To use the name of the file being processed in *cmd*, use { } to represent this argument. If *cmd* does not return true (the value 0), no remaining options are processed. This option is confusing until you see an example; one just happens to follow in a few paragraphs.

Other options are available for `find`, including options to join and negate other options. Consult your *UNIX Reference Manual* for more information.

Here are some examples to show you how to use `find`. To create a list of all regular files in the directory `/usr/man`, use this command:

```
$ find /usr/man -type f -print ⏎
```

The first option (`-type` f) is true only for regular files, and false for directories and other file types. Any files that pass this test proceed to the next option (-print), which sends the name of the file to stdout.

The next example removes the files in /tmp and /usr/tmp that have not changed in more than five days:

```
$ find /tmp /usr/tmp -mtime +5 -exec rm {} \; ↵
```

If the file does not pass the -mtime test, the -exec option does not execute, and the file is not removed. This example executes silently; to display each file as it is removed, change the command to this:

```
$ find /tmp /usr/tmp -mtime +5 -print -exec rm {} \; ↵
```

The -print option is specified before the -exec option so you can see the name of the file before it is removed. If rm fails, you will know which file could not be removed because an error message will appear after the filename in the output.

Back to Looping

Now that you know about find, let's discuss one more example for loop:

```
for files in `find . -type f -print`
do
    result=`grep "$1" $files`
    if [ -n "$result" ]
    then
        echo ${files}:
        echo "$result"
    fi
done
```

In this example, grep is used to search each regular file in the current directory and any of its subdirectories for the string specified as the first argument (*$1*) to this script. If the string is found in the file, the results from the grep command are displayed.

Why not just do

```
$ grep string `find . -type f -print`
```

where *string* is the pattern to match? Because the list of files that find generates may be too long for the shell to handle. If so, you will receive the message:

```
Too many arguments.
```

Another type of loop, the `while` loop, executes a list of commands while a certain condition is true. The syntax for this loop is as follows:

```
while condition
do
    commands
done
```

In this command, the condition is the same as a conditional comparison used by the `if` command. If the condition is true, then the commands execute. Once the commands finish executing, the condition is evaluated again; if the condition is still true, the commands execute again. This process continues until the condition becomes false, at which time the loop terminates.

For example, you can define a script named `ll` to perform the following commands:

```
while [ -n "$1" ]
do
    ls -lF $1
    shift
done
```

In this example, if a value is found in *$1*, the command `ls -lF` is executed on this positional parameter and then the arguments are shifted. This loop executes as long as a value is found in *$1*.

The converse of this loop is the `until` loop, which executes a set of commands until a specified condition occurs. The `until` syntax is similar to the `while` syntax; you could rewrite the above example like this:

```
until [ -z "$1" ]
do
    ls -lF $1
    shift
done
```

You can use two special shell commands, `break` and `continue`, inside `do`/`done` blocks. If you must prematurely terminate a `for`, `while`, or `until` loop, use `break`. The syntax for `break` is

```
break n
```

where *n*, if specified, is the number of nested `for`, `while`, and `until` loops to terminate. For example, if you are within a `for` loop nested within a `while` loop, to terminate both loops and continue executing after the `done` statement for the `while` loop, execute `break 2`. If *n* is not specified, the default is 1.

While you are processing the commands within a loop, if you want to jump directly to the `done` statement (and, subsequently, back to the *loop_control* statement), execute the `continue` command.

Defining Functions

When creating a Bourne shell script, you may need to define functions. A function is a way to divide a script's task into bite-sized morsels. Functions also let you create the Bourne shell equivalent of C shell's aliases.

A function is defined as

```
name() {commands;}
```

where *name* is the name of the function and *commands* is the list of commands to execute when *name* is executed. A function defined in this manner is similar to a miniscript. For example, within a function, positional parameters refer only to the command-line arguments you specified when you invoked the function.

Let's create an example function to perform `ls -1F`:

```
$ ll() { ↵
>    echo "- Long File Listing -" ↵
>    ls -1F $*; ↵
>    } ↵
$ _
```

The right angle bracket (>) is your secondary shell prompt, which appears whenever a shell command requires more information to complete a command. The *PS2* environment variable defines this prompt, which you can change in the same manner as the *PS1* environment variable.

NOTE: You must terminate the last command in a function with a semicolon.

Once you have defined the function, invoke it:

```
$ ll /usr ⏎
```

The difference between defining a function and creating a script is that a function is local to your shell or your shell script and is not visible to any other user; on the other hand, anyone who can access a shell script can execute it. Functions also tend to execute faster.

Because functions are similar to local variables, you can use the set command to view the functions you have defined:

```
$ set ⏎
HOME=/users/demobsh
LOGNAME=demobsh
MAIL=/usr/spool/mail/demobsh
PATH=/bin:/usr/bin:/users/demobsh/bin:.
PS1=$
PS2=>
TERM=vt100
TZ=EST5EDT
ll(){
echo "- Long File Listing -"
ls -lF $*
}
$ _
```

Use functions within shell scripts when you want to define a complicated task to execute multiple nonsuccessive times. You must define the function in the script before you can reference it. Once you have defined the function, reference it the same as you would reference any UNIX command.

If you want to define a set of functions to use interactively, add their definitions to your .profile file. Each time you log in, these functions will be available.

Functions return values depending on the success or failure of the function, similar to the way programs return values. You can use this value either as a comparison in test, case, or if commands or as the control for while or until loops.

To return a value from your function, include the command

```
return n
```

where the value returned is *n*; if you do not specify *n*, the return value is obtained from the last command the function executed.

When a `return` statement executes, the function immediately terminates. The invoking script or shell can obtain the return value via the parameter `$?`. Remember, `return` 0 when the function successfully completes; use nonzero values for unsuccessful returns.

Other Bourne Shell Programming Commands

Finally, to round out the tricks you can perform with Bourne shell scripts and functions, some additional commands to provide more flexibility in your programming.

Just as functions use `return` to exit and return a value, `exit` terminates a shell script and returns a value. The syntax for this command is

```
exit n
```

where the value returned is *n*; if *n* is not specified, the `exit` value is obtained from the last command the script executed. As with `return`, the `exit` value is placed into *$?*.

If you want to add a pause to your script, use `sleep(1)`, which causes the script to wait a specific number of seconds before continuing with the next command in the script.

Another shell command that provides many useful features is `set`. I have already described how to use `set` to copy a variable into the positional parameters. You also can use `set` to control certain options for executing the script. Table 9-2 shows some of the options for `set`.

Table 9-2. Options for the `set` Command

Option	Use
e	Exit immediately from the script if a command exits with a nonzero return value.
n	Check the syntax for a shell script, but do not execute it.

Table 9-2. Options for the set *Command (continued)*

Option	Use
x	Display each command and its arguments from the script as the command is executed.

Precede these options with a minus sign to start the option. Precede an option with a plus sign to stop the option. Once an option starts, it continues until either the script terminates or the option is stopped.

The most useful set command is:

```
set -x
```

This command usually is placed into a shell script to assist in debugging a script or function.

One final command you can use when creating a shell script is read. The read command solicits a line of text from stdin, assigning the values read into one or more shell variables. The syntax for this command is

```
read [ var1 [ var2 [ ... ] ]
```

where *var1* and *var2* are shell variables. The brackets indicate only that *var1* and *var2* are optional. Read places the first word read into *var1*, the second word into *var2*, and so on. If more words are entered than variables to receive, all leftover words are assigned to the last variable in the list. If you specify no variables, the information read from stdin is lost.

A quick example of read:

```
echo "Continue?  Enter y or n\c"
read answer
case $answer in
  [Nn]*) exit 0;;
  *) ;;
esac
```

This example prompts you for y or n, which may be entered either in uppercase or lowercase. If you enter n, the script exits; otherwise, the script continues.

C SHELL PROGRAMMING

In some instances, a C shell script is easier to create than a Bourne shell script to perform the same function. Mostly, these advantages are based on C shell's intrinsic numerical capabilities and the ability to reference specific words in a list.

In most instances, however, you should use Bourne shell commands to create your scripts. You can port Bourne shell scripts to any UNIX machine. The C shell is still not available with all UNIX implementations.

This section primarily discusses the differences between programming with Bourne shell commands and programming with C shell commands.

Shell Arguments and Other Parameters

In addition to the variables *$cwd* (current directory) and *$status* (last exit value), the C shell includes another built-in variable, *$argv*, to provide all command-line arguments (similar to *$**).

As with the Bourne shell, you can access each command-line argument using the positional parameters (for example, *$0* is the program's name), and `$$` contains the current process identification number. You also may `shift` the arguments, as with the Bourne shell.

In the C shell, however, you can access each word of a variable independently, without first assigning the variable to the positional parameters. To reference a single word in a variable, use the syntax

```
$varname[idx]
```

where *idx* is the number of the word within *varname* you want to access; each word is separated by at least one space or tab. The first word of a variable is numbered 1. You also may select a range of words by specifying the start and stop index separated by a minus sign. For example, `$var[3-5]` indicates words 3, 4, and 5 of the variable *var*. You also may use these constructs when accessing a numerical variable.

To obtain the number of words assigned to a variable, use the notation `$#varname`, where *varname* is the name of the variable.

The following commands illustrate:

```
120> set files = `find /usr/bin -print`
121> echo $#files
```

```
229
122> echo $files[22] ↵
/usr/bin/tic
123> _
```

Event 120 sets the variable `files` to the list of files and directories that `find`(*1*) generates. Event 121 echoes the number of files and directories in the list. Event 122 displays the twenty-second word in this list.

If you select word 240 of `files`, the shell returns this error message:

```
Subscript out of range.
```

The C shell has a special variable, *$<*, that reads a line from stdin. For example, to prompt for and read a single line of text, you can use the following:

```
echo -n "Continue? Enter y or n"
set answer = $<
```

In this example, the line of text read from stdin is placed in the local variable `answer`.

More on Conditional Comparisons

The `case` construct in the Bourne shell also is available in the C shell, but it has a different syntax. The C shell command, `switch`, has the following syntax:

```
switch(string)
    case pattern1:
        commands_1
        breaksw
    case pattern2:
        commands_2
        breaksw
    .
    .
    .
    default:
        commands_default
        breaksw
endsw
```

The `switch` construct looks a little more complex than the `case` command, but it contains the same basic pieces of information. The `breaksw` command has the same function as the double semicolon in Bourne shell scripts—to separate one choice's actions from another. However, `breaksw` is not required at the end of each choice's actions; the Bourne shell does require the double semicolon.

In the above construct, *pattern* strings are matched according to the shell wildcard rules (see Chapter 2). Once *string*, which may be a variable or a word from a variable, matches a pattern, the associated set of UNIX or C shell commands executes until either `breaksw` or `endsw` is reached. You can specify multiple patterns for one set of commands as follows:

```
switch (string)
   case pattern1:
   case pattern2:
      commands_1
      breaksw
endsw
```

If the string matches either *pattern1* or *pattern2*, *commands_1* execute. This construct is similar to the Bourne shell use of the or (|) operator in a `case` pattern.

The `default` case executes only if no *pattern* matches *string*.

Time for an exercise: Convert the `case` examples shown earlier in this chapter to `switch` commands.

Looping

Looping in the C shell differs only slightly from looping in the Bourne shell. The `for` and `while` constructs have slightly different syntaxes, and `until` does not exist (but then again, do you really need it?).

In the C shell, the `while` loop has the following syntax:

```
while ( condition )
   commands
end
```

While *condition* is true, *commands* are repeatedly executed; *condition* has the same syntax as the conditional comparisons used with the `if` statement.

The C shell equivalent to the Bourne shell `for` command is the command `foreach`, which has the following syntax:

```
foreach var (list)
    commands
end
```

The commands between the `foreach` and the `end` statements are executed for each word in *list*. Each time through the loop, the next word from *list* is assigned to *var*. *List* is usually a variable, such as `$argv`.

As with the Bourne shell, you may use both the `break` and `continue` commands to control the execution of a C shell loop.

Nothing is really new in this section, so I haven't included any examples. If you want to practice, try converting the Bourne shell looping examples in the first half of this chapter to the C shell format.

Other C Shell Programming Commands

As before, this is the catch-all section, containing C shell commands that just don't fit into any other section.

For all you shell programmers out there who really want to create spaghetti code, the `goto` command is available. The syntax for this command is:

```
goto string
    .
    .
    .
label:
    commands
```

Basically, *string* may be a variable name, an element of a variable, or a quoted string of characters. The shell interprets the value for *string*, and a `label` within the program must exactly match the text for *string*. Execution then continues with the commands following this `label`. The `label:` must be the only command on its line.

Like the Bourne shell, the C shell provides `exit` and `echo`; however, an `exit` value may be any C shell numerical expression, and `echo` uses the `-n` option to suppress the automatic linefeed.

The C shell `set` command does not provide options similar to those of the

Bourne shell set command. However, you can perform the Bourne shell set -x command by using the C shell command set echo.

AUTOMATICALLY EDITING FILES WITH SPELLING ERRORS

At the beginning of this chapter, I proposed the problem of editing a set of files containing spelling errors. Below is the Bourne shell script to check the spelling for a set of files (passed as arguments to the script) and edit the files containing errors:

```
: /bin/sh
#
# This script checks a list of files, passed as arguments,
# and shows you any spelling errors and then permits you to
# edit the file (if you have write permission) to correct
# these errors.
#
PATH=/bin:/usr/bin:/usr/ucb
export PATH

# If no args, exit.
if [ $# -eq 0 ]
then
     echo "No files to check.  Exiting.\n"
     exit 0
fi

#
# For each file, check the spelling and display any errors
#
for check_file
do
     if [ -f $check_file -a -r $check_file ]
     then
         errors="`spell $check_file 2>&1`"

         #
         # If any errors found, let user view them and then edit
         # the file IF DESIRED.
         #
```

```
        if [ -n "$errors" ]
        then
            echo "$check_file contains errors.  Display them? \c"
            read response
            case $response in
                [yY]*) echo "$errors" | more ;;
                    *) ;;
            esac

            if [ -w $check_file ]
            then
                #
                # If user wants to edit, get editor from EDITOR
                # variable, if assigned; otherwise, use vi.
                #
                echo "Do you want to edit $check_file? \c"
                read response
                case $response in
                    [yY]*)
                            if [ -x "$EDITOR" ]
                            then
                                $EDITOR $check_file
                            else
                                vi $check_file
                            fi
                            ;;
                        *) ;;
                esac
            else
                echo "You do not have permission to write to this file."
            fi
        fi
    fi
done
```

If you create such a script, remember to make it executable. Also remember not to place a pound sign (#) in the first column of the script's first line.

I'll leave converting this example to use C shell commands as an exercise for you.

ONWARD...

Well, that's it: You now know enough about UNIX to converse about it knowledgeably and to use it proficiently and confidently. The thoughts and tips in this book are intended to show you not only how to use the operating system, but how to master some of its more useful features.

Finally, if you want to explore some other UNIX commands, investigate the commands diff, cmp, pg, bc, and tee, documented in Section 1 of your *UNIX Reference Manual*.

Good luck on your UNIX journey.

Glossary

account — Your user environment. You must enter (log in to) it to access your UNIX system.

account name — The name assigned to your account. Use this name to obtain access to the system.

alias — A string that represents one or more commands. Aliases are available in the C shell and the Korn shell.

background — The appropriate execution state for most time-consuming processes. The shell does not wait for a background process to complete before issuing another shell prompt; foreground processes must complete before the shell will issue another prompt. When executing a task, append an ampersand to place the task into the background.

bit bucket — The place where all bits in your system go to die. Once a day your system administrator must empty this bucket. *See also* /dev/null.

blind copy (bcc) list — The list of those who receive an electronic mail message without other recipients' knowledge.

boot — The act of starting your system.

Bourne shell — One of the shells available with your UNIX system. The Bourne shell is the standard shell provided with all UNIX systems. It's also the least appealing shell to use.

buffer (vi) — A named or numbered storage area where you can put deleted and yanked text for later retrieval. You must precede buffer names with a double quote and follow them with a command, either d, y, p, or P.

buffer history stack — The numbered vi buffers organized into a stack containing the last nine deleted items.

built-in variables — The C shell term for shell parameters. These variables have names like *$status* and *$argv*. Only the shell can assign values to built-in variables.

carbon copy (cc) list — The list of secondary recipients of an electronic mail message. All recipients of the message receive the carbon copy list of other recipients.

colon command — A vi command that begins with a colon. Colon commands also are known as ex commands, since they are the same as those used by the ex editor. An example is the substitution command, :s.

command arguments — The information and options you specify for a command. For example, in the command ls /bin, the command argument is /bin; ls is the command's name.

command history — The list of commands executed from the current shell. The C and Korn shells provide a command history.

conditional comparison — A test to determine whether something is true or not. Conditional comparisons are used during shell programming. Different actions may be taken on the basis of the result of the comparison. Conditional comparisons are used with the shell programming constructs if, while, and until.

crontab file — The file containing the list of commands that cron periodically executes. Create your crontab file using vi and run crontab(1) to register it.

C shell — One of the shells available with your UNIX system. The C shell was developed at the University of California at Berkeley and comes with many versions of UNIX, including release 4. The C shell has several interactive features that improve on the operating environment of the Bourne shell; if it is available, you should use the C shell as your login shell.

.cshrc — The C shell initialization (start-up) script. This script executes each time a C shell starts. This file, which you create and maintain, resides in your home directory.

dead letter — The file containing an interrupted electronic message. If you do not finish writing an electronic mail message, mailx creates a dead letter file for the message's contents.

device file — The file that provides access to a system peripheral or other physical system resource.

/dev/null — The device file where you can redirect output if you do not want it. Also known as the UNIX bit bucket. *See also* bit bucket.

directory — A file-grouping mechanism. Within UNIX, a directory is also considered a file containing a list of the files in the directory.

/ **directory** — *See* root directory.

electronic mail — The facility, part of all UNIX systems, that permits you to route text messages to other users either on your system or on a system connected to yours.

electronic mailbox — The file containing your electronic mail. Read this file using mailx.

e-mail — *See* electronic mail.

environment variables — Shell variables whose values are available to any command subsequently executed from the shell. In the Bourne shell, you create an environment variable by exporting it; in the C shell, you use setenv to create environment variables.

escaping — The act of overriding a metacharacter's or wildcard's magic properties. To escape a metacharacter or wildcard, precede it with a backslash.

/etc/profile — The systemwide Bourne shell initialization script. Your system administrator creates and maintains this script. It executes before your .profile each time a Bourne shell starts.

event — A command or set of commands the shell executes. Both the C shell and the Korn shell place each event executed on a command history stack.

execute access — The permission controlling whether a file can be executed. Owner, group, and world (all other users) are the three levels of execute access. Use chmod(1) to control file permission.

expanded memory — A DOS memory standard that permits programs to access memory above the 640-KB limit. Expanded memory, also called banked memory, is very slow for most applications.

export **(shell variables)** — The Bourne shell command to change a local variable into an environment variable.

.exrc — Your vi configuration file. This file resides in your home directory and contains ex (colon) commands that you want to execute each time you start vi. In most instances, only the :set and :map commands are placed into this file.

extended memory — A DOS memory standard that permits programs to access memory above the 640-KB limit. Extended memory is quicker than expanded memory.

file descriptor — The numerical value the operating system assigns to a file when the file is opened. The operating system uses this descriptor for all subsequent accesses to the file. By default, all processes open standard input (descriptor 0), standard output (descriptor 1), and standard error (descriptor 2).

file owner — The user who creates a file. This ownership attribute controls who can change the file's permissions with chmod(*1*).

file permission — An attribute controlling access to a file. The three types of file permissions each have three levels of permission. The permission types are read access, write access, and execute access. The three levels of permission are owner, group, and world.

foreground — The execution state for most processes. Your shell waits for the completion of a foreground process before issuing another prompt. You may execute long processes in the background; the shell does not wait for a background process to complete before issuing another prompt.

full pathname — A filename specification that includes all directories beginning with the root directory. For example, /usr/bin/vi is a full pathname.

function — A shell module that can be executed like a command yet is local to the current shell or shell script.

group permission — Access permitted to a file by a defined group. Use chmod(*1*) to control which types of access are permitted. If you are the file's owner, use chgrp(*1*) to control which group has access to the file.

header summary (mailx) — When you start mailx, it displays the header summary to show you what messages are in your electronic mailbox.

history stack — The list of commands you have executed in the current C or Korn shell. The most recently executed command is at the bottom of the stack.

home directory — The directory you automatically enter when you log in to the system.

host — Your computer.

hot-key program — A DOS program that resides in memory and is activated by a predefined interrupt (such as by pressing a keyboard key). Also known as a terminate-and-stay-resident (TSR) program.

job — A set of processes grouped as one task.

job control — The facility, provided with the C and Korn shells, that lets you change the state of a job. The possible states for any job are foreground, background, and suspended.

job number — The number that the shell assigns to a job. Multiple processes, if grouped as a single job, are assigned a single job number.

kernel — The main programs governing all activities on a UNIX system.

keyboard mapping — Typing shortcuts in vi. You can assign commands to be executed when you press certain keys. Use the vi command :map.

kismet — Fate, destiny. I like this term better than *bug*.

Korn shell — The newest shell. Included with release 4 of UNIX, it combines features from both the Bourne shell and the C shell. The result is an incredibly complex shell that many users seem to like.

link — An alternative name for a file. Create file links using ln(1). *See also* symbolic link.

link count — The number of filenames representing a single file. The link count for a file can be displayed with the ls -l command.

local variable — A shell variable that you have not exported; the values for local variables are available only to the current shell or shell script, not to any commands subsequently executed.

log in — To attain access to the system. After you negotiate the login sequence by entering your account name and password, you are logged in.

.login — The C shell start-up script that executes immediately following .cshrc if the C shell is your login shell. This file, which you create and maintain, resides in your home directory.

login messages — The system messages that appear when you log in to a system.

login name — *See* account name.

log out — The act of leaving a system. To log out of any shell, use the `exit` command.

`.logout` — The C shell termination script. This script, which executes only when you exit your login C shell, contains the final commands for your shell to execute. This file, which you create and maintain, is located in your home directory.

magic — The property granted to certain characters within `vi` in order to create a regular expression (RE). Without magic, these characters are mortal and can be killed.

`.mailrc` — The electronic mail configuration file, containing commands to tailor `mailx`. This file, which you create and maintain, resides in your home directory.

manpage — *See* manual page.

manual page — An entry in the *UNIX Reference Manual* for a specific command.

marker (`vi`) — A bookmark that you can temporarily attach to a specific character of a file while editing the file with `vi`. Markers are created using the `m` (marker) command; to reference a marker, precede the marker name with a single quote or a grave mark.

mbox — Your secondary electronic mailbox. Electronic mail messages are initially stored in your primary mailbox (*see* electronic mailbox). You can transfer messages from the primary mailbox to any secondary mailbox.

metacharacter — A character endowed with magic properties. A metacharacter can represent other characters or groups of characters. Escape a metacharacter to make it a normal character.

multitasking—The ability of an operating system to manage multiple unrelated processes.

named buffer — A `vi` buffer named by one of the 26 letters of the alphabet. Named buffers retain their value while you remain in `vi`.

named pipe — A device file that acts like a pipe.

numbered buffer — A vi buffer referenced with a number from one through nine. Numbered buffers are organized into a history stack for storing multiple unnamed deletions.

owner permission — A file owner's ability to read, write, and execute the file. Control access to a file with chmod(1).

paging — The process of moving sections of program code and data between the system's memory and its swap area on the disk. Paging is so called because each section that is moved is a page.

password — The secret code required to gain access to a computer account.

peripherals — The external devices, such as terminals and printers, connected to your system.

pipe — The system resource that permits you to use the output from one program as the input for another. Create a pipe by placing a vertical bar (|) between the commands you want to connect. Always place the command whose output you are piping before the pipe symbol.

positional parameters — The shell parameters that contain the first nine arguments specified when the shell script was executed. The parameter *$0* contains the name of the shell script; the parameters *$1* through *$9* contain the first nine arguments. Use shift to reference any script arguments beyond the ninth.

primary group — One of the groups to which your system administrator assigns your account. The other members of this group may access any files you create if the file's group permissions authorize group access.

process — An executing program. Each process is identified by its process identification number.

process identifier (PID) number — The number the system assigns to identify each process running in the system.

.profile — The Bourne shell start-up script. It executes whenever a Bourne shell starts. This file, which you create and maintain, resides in your home directory.

RAM — Random access memory. Your system's internal memory.

read access — The permission controlling whether a file can be read. The three levels of read access are owner, group, and world. Control file permission with chmod(*1*).

real-time UNIX — A term applied to systems that can grant priority to a more important task, regardless of the task's nature, at the expense of other tasks in the system.

recursive — A person who repeatedly uses the same four-letter word. Okay, I lied. This term, used with the rm command, indicates that the command first removes the contents of a directory and then removes the directory. A better term would be *depth-first deletion*, but this phrase is too wrapped in graph theory for general acceptance.

redirection — The act of rerouting output destined for stdout or stderr or the act of providing another source of data to fulfill the standard input requirements of a program.

regular expression (RE) — A search pattern. You may specify it either as a search or substitution string within vi or as a search string for grep(*1*) and several other UNIX utilities.

regular file — Just your normal program or text file. Any file that is not a directory, symbolic link, named pipe, or device file is considered regular.

relative pathname — A filename specification based on the user's current directory location. For example, the filename ../bin/trust is a relative pathname.

root directory — The topmost directory in your UNIX system. Unlike DOS, which has a unique root directory on every disk partition, you have only one of these directories at all times.

root disk — The primary disk in your system, the one containing the root directory.

search access — The permission controlling whether you can view a directory's contents. The three levels of search access are owner, group, and world. Chmod(*1*) controls file permission.

secondary shell prompt — The prompt the shell displays when it expects more information to complete the current command.

shell — A command processor.

shell parameters — Read-only shell variables that you can access to obtain information about the shell or about the last command the shell or shell script executed.

shell programming — The act of creating shell scripts.

shell prompt — The characters displayed by the shell to indicate that it is ready for the next command.

shell script — A file containing a sequence of shell commands organized to perform a set of tasks. A shell program.

shell variable — A storage area maintained by the shell, used either to configure your shell or to store information for later use.

shut down — To stop all executing processes. Before you can turn off the power on a UNIX system, you must shut down the system.

stderr — Standard error. The normal location for error messages a program generates.

stdin — Standard input. The normal location from which to obtain input for a program.

stdout — Standard output. The location to which a program normally routes informational, status, and prompt messages.

superuser — The system administrator's account on the system. Also known as *root*.

suspend (job) — The act of temporarily halting a process without removing the process from the system.

swap area — The area on your disk that the system uses to store pages of program code or data not presently needed.

swap out — The act of removing one or more pages of a program's code or data from the system memory and, optionally, copying these pages into the swap area.

swapping — The process cf moving pages of program code or data between the swap area and system memory.

symbolic link — A file that provides an alternate filename for another file. A symbolic link may cross physical disks or systems on a network.

task priority — The numerical value assigned to all processes. The operating system uses it to determine which process runs next.

task scheduling — The process of adjusting the priority for any tasks in the system and for running the highest-priority task next. This system is responsible for performing these activities.

the brick — The *UNIX Reference Manual.*

tilde commands — Commands you can execute while creating an electronic message in mailx. These commands must begin in column one of the message and begin with a tilde.

time slice — The portion of CPU time allotted to a process. During an allotted time slice no other process may use the CPU.

tty — Your terminal's interface to the UNIX system. Pronounced tee-tee-why.

UNIX Reference Manual — The most important manuals in your documentation. They describe every command available to you. These manuals also may be named the *User's Reference Manual* and the *Programmer's Reference Manual.*

unnamed buffer — The default vi buffer for the text most recently yanked or deleted. If you don't use a named buffer, the text is placed into the unnamed buffer, and you can access it with the p or P command without preceding the command with a named buffer reference. You also can access the unnamed buffer as buffer 1.

user group — Most often, a group of people who work closely together, such as a department. When the administrator creates a user's account, he or she assigns the user membership in one or more user groups. *See* group permission.

username — *See* account name.

vi — The standard UNIX full-screen editor. Pronounced vee-eye.

vi **internal work area** — The area vi uses to store your file while you make changes. You must save this work area to disk using the :w command before exiting vi, or your changes will be lost.

virtual memory operating system — An operating system that provides a scheme that permits programs to access more memory than physically available on the system. Since the memory is not real, it is considered virtual.

wildcard — A character that can be used to match one or more other characters. Shell wildcards include * (to match any number of characters) and ? (to match a single character).

world permission — This permission level determines who outside of the file's owner and group may access a particular file and how. Also called *other permission*.

write access — The permission controlling whether you can write into a given file or whether you can create a file in a given directory. The three levels of write access are owner, group, and world. The file owner or the system administrator controls file permission with chmod(*1*).

Index

C

G

H

I

J

N

T

U